PENGUIN CLASSICS

THE TREASURE OF THE CITY OF LADIES

Christine de Pisan was one of the most remarkable and respected literary figures in the courts of medieval Europe, the more so for being the only professional woman writer of her time. She was born in Venice in 1365, but while she was still a child her family left Italy and went to the court of Charles V of France, where her father, Thomas de Pizzano, was court physician and astrologer. When she was fifteen years old she married the young nobleman and courtier Étienne de Castel. Her happiness was marred first by the death of Charles V in 1380, which led to Thomas de Pizzano's demotion, then by the latter's illness and death only a few years later. In 1390 Étienne de Castel also died suddenly, leaving his young widow with three children, her mother and a niece to support. Christine de Pisan now turned to writing and soon secured an enviable reputation for her lyric poetry. She went on to write with great success on moral issues; two major concerns were the need for peace and the role of women in society, but she also wrote with authority on public affairs and the art of government, as well as producing a highly acclaimed biography of Charles V. Her output was vast and she incorporated many autobiographical details into her poetry, making it an invaluable record of medieval life. Much of her work survives in lavishly illuminated manuscripts, for she enjoyed influential patronage throughout her career. The outbreak of civil war in France prompted her to take refuge in a convent in 1418, where she remained until her death some time after 1429.

Sarah Lawson was born in Indianapolis in 1943 and studied at Indiana University and Glasgow University, where she took a Ph.D. in English in 1971. In 1979–80 she held a C. Day Lewis Fellowship in creative writing, awarded by the Greater London Arts Association. She is a writer, reviewer and translator, and lives in London.

Christine de Pisan

THE TREASURE
OF THE CITY OF LADIES

or

The Book of the Three Virtues

TRANSLATED WITH AN INTRODUCTION BY
SARAH LAWSON

PENGUIN BOOKS

PENGUIN BOOKS

Published by the Penguin Group
27 Wrights Lane, London w8 5TZ, England
Viking Penguin Inc., 40 West 23rd Street, New York, New York 10010, USA
Penguin Books Australia Ltd, Ringwood, Victoria, Australia
Penguin Books Canada Ltd, 2801 John Street, Markham, Ontario, Canada L3R 1B4
Penguin Books (NZ) Ltd, 182–190 Wairau Road, Auckland 10, New Zealand

Penguin Books Ltd, Registered Offices: Harmondsworth, Middlesex, England

This translation first published 1985
5 7 9 10 8 6

Made and printed in Great Britain by
Richard Clay Ltd, Bungay, Suffolk
Filmset in Monophoto Photina

Dedicated to the memory of
my mother,
Fern Reed Lawson (later Hadley)
1902–81

TABLE OF CONTENTS

7

PART TWO

ACKNOWLEDGEMENTS

I wish to thank the authorities of the Bibliothèque Nationale in Paris and the British Library in London for their help and cooperation in allowing me to see various manuscripts and early printed versions of *Le Livre du Trésor de la Cité des Dames* in their possession. I also wish to thank Dr Monika Jafri and Katherine Ivens, who have given me their support and advice and have shared their enthusiasm for Christine with me, and Alastair Pettigrew and Hazel Brothers, who have helped me with their interest and encouragement.

INTRODUCTION

There cannot have been many writers who have been publicly 'discovered' as often as Christine de Pisan (1365–1430?). In her own lifetime and for the century after her death she was a respected writer on moral questions, education, the art of government, the conduct of war, and the life and times of Charles V. She was a skilled poet and a courageous fighter for justice. Although she was an early and outstanding *femme de lettres* in France and the first professional woman writer in Europe, by the seventeenth century hardly anyone had heard of her. She was discovered briefly in the early 1600s and there was a plan to publish some of her works, but the scheme came to nothing. In the eighteenth century she was discovered again by Jean Boivin de Villeneuve, who published an account of her life in 1717. Voltaire had heard of her, but thought her name was Catherine. In 1786 Louise Guinement de Kéralio included extracts and summaries of Christine's writings in her ambitious series of the best work of women authors in France. Raymond Thomassy praised her enthusiastically in 1838 in his *Essay on the Political Writings of Christine de Pisan*, and fifty years later there was a flurry of scholarship devoted to Christine when her lyric poetry was finally printed and the letters in the *Querelle* (debate) of the *Romance of the Rose* were edited. But by 1911 a feminist scholar, Rose Rigaud, was complaining that there were still no modern editions of Christine's major prose works. Some of the titles she wished to see in accessible editions remain unedited and unpublished to this day.

Since the early part of this century Christine de Pisan seems to have been poised on the brink of recognition and 'classic' status without ever quite joining the pantheon. Although in her own lifetime her contemporaries apparently judged her writings on their merits, some later critics have been misled by their own prejudices. In 1924 one male historian of French literature dismissed Christine as a mediocre bluestocking. Another modern French anthologist speaks slightingly of her *prolixité toute feminine* (a very odd remark to make about a writer of the Middle Ages, when prolixity was the fashion). Still another editor of a recent survey of scholarship of medieval French literature remarks dismissively that most of the interest in Christine has been shown by members of her own sex, as though that discredits the whole enterprise.

It seems possible that if Christine had been merely a remarkable medieval writer instead of a remarkable medieval woman writer she might not have had to be discovered and rediscovered quite so many times. She might have been an accepted classic long before this, taking her place beside the other writers who represent that period. She is still best known as a lyric poet, perhaps because her poetry was edited as long ago as 1886 by Maurice Roy, but her prose works remain largely neglected. A few of her poems can be found in anthologies of French poetry, and a few paragraphs from her *Letter to the God of Love* may appear in textbook collections of medieval prose, but for such a prolific writer of such importance in her own time she is astonishingly under-represented in modern anthologies and editions. Some of her works, like *The Treasure of the City of Ladies* (last printed in 1536 in French), have never been issued in a modern French edition and have never been translated into English before. Christine's work is now in an exciting category of literature that is 'classic' in the sense that it is worth reading as a representation of the life and experience of another epoch, but not quite yet 'classic' in the sense that is widely known and quoted.

CHRISTINE'S LIFE

Much is known of Christine de Pisan's family and early life, thanks to her autobiographical writings. Her father was Thomas de Pizzano, a noted physician and astrologer in Bologna. He married the daughter of his colleague, Thomas Mondini. Both Thomas Mondini and his son-in-law became counsellors to the government of Venice, and it was there that Christine was born in 1365. The reputation of Thomas de Pizzano grew to such an extent that he received invitations from Louis I of Hungary and Charles V of France to come to their courts. Thomas chose France because of the humanist reputation of its king, his splendid court, and the fame of the University of Paris. Thomas visited the court of Charles V, leaving his wife and children in Bologna. After a year, the king refused to let him leave but offered to pay the travelling expenses of his family to join him in Paris.

One December day, as Christine recounts it in *The Vision of Christine*, Thomas's little daughter, dressed in the exotic clothing of Lombardy, was presented at the Louvre to the kindly Charles V, whose biography she was to write nearly thirty-five years later at the request of his brother Phillip the Bold, Duke of Burgundy.

Christine de Pisan* spent the rest of her life in France, in spite of invitations she had at the height of her fame from Henry IV of England and the Duke of Milan to grace their courts. The education she had at the hands of her enlightened father must have been unique for a girl in the fourteenth century. She could read French and Italian and probably Latin, although she seems to have relied on French translations of Latin authors. Later, when she applied herself to a period of serious independent study, she already had the tools of literacy at her disposal.

Her father enjoyed great success at the French court. In addition to being the physician and astrologer to the king, he became a trusted adviser on state matters. His advice does not seem to have been notably shrewd, but Charles V thought him indispensable. The king showered him with gifts and promises of gifts in addition to his salary as court astrologer; during the lucrative 1370s Thomas was presented with money, property and annual incomes.

When Christine reached marriageable age, she was much sought after because of the royal favour shown her father. The choice of a husband was made by Thomas, not Christine, but nevertheless the marriage was, or turned into, a love-match. In 1380, at fifteen, she married Étienne de (or du) Castel, a young nobleman from Picardy. He was a promising courtier and became the king's secretary and notary. At the end of the 1370s, just when the families of de Pisan and de Castel were enjoying an apparently secure prosperity, disaster struck. Charles V died at forty-four on 16 September 1380. Christine later wrote: 'Now the door to our misfortunes was open, and I, being still quite young, entered in.' The various pensions provided by the king were abruptly withdrawn and Thomas's salary was cut. His family had lived well but now they fell on hard times. In her literary work Christine often uses the popular medieval image of Dame Fortune and her wheel; one may be enjoying great prosperity and good luck, but with a half revolution of the wheel even kings may descend to

---

*Her gallicized name is sometimes written *Pizan*. It was at one time thought that she must have been from Pisa, but the name derives from Pizzano, a town near Bologna.

the depths of misery. For Christine it was an allegorical expression of her own reality, not merely a literary device.

Thomas de Pisan himself died, after much ill-health, some time between 1385 and 1390. Étienne de Castel, now the head of his father-in-law's household, travelled to Beauvais with King Charles VI in the autumn of 1390 and there caught some sort of contagious disease and quickly died. Now, at twenty-five, a grief-stricken widow with three children, her mother and a niece to support, Christine saw her position on Fortune's wheel drop to its lowest level. Later, when she began to write, she feelingly described the plight of the widow and the problems of protracted lawsuits concerning inheritance.

Faced with debts and living expenses for six, what was Christine to do? What ways of making a living were open to a woman in 1390? Remarriage would have been one way out, but for whatever reason, Christine did not choose it. Entering a convent (as she was later to do in her fifties) would have kept a roof over her head, but it would not have benefited the rest of her family. Had her husband had a trade or business she might have continued it herself, but her husband had not been a tradesman. If she had been the country-bred wife of a peasant farmer, she might have supported her family by toil on the land. In *The Treasure of the City of Ladies* she suggests doing laundry as a respectable occupation for a woman, but it is unlikely that she considered it for herself.

As relief from the cares of a penurious widowhood (at one time she had four lawsuits running concurrently), Christine applied herself to study. She began at the beginning – like a child, she said, learning its ABC – with histories of the world, histories of the Hebrews, Assyrians, famous rulers of antiquity, the Romans, then the French and Bretons. As well as all the history she could find, she read widely in science and poetry. Armed with this learning, Christine began to write. Fortunately, her first efforts, conventional love *ballades* and other lyrical forms, the earliest composed around 1393, met with considerable success, and she was encouraged to continue writing. By the end of the decade she was writing seriously for a living. She seems to have gradually fallen into the profession of letters, writing partly for pleasure and partly from financial necessity, a daring way of life, unheard of for a woman of her time.

The autobiographical content of her works makes her remarkable in the Middle Ages, when writers wrote and rewrote versions of popular stories, but revealed very few personal details. *The Changes of Fortune*

(*La Mutacion de Fortune*, finished in November 1403) is an immensely long poem of 23,636 lines in which she describes the reversals in her own life and then shows how the vagaries of Fortune have affected others. She includes some striking vignettes of contemporary life and then continues with a wide-ranging history of the world. At the same time Christine was composing various short poems and *The Epistle of Othea*, a collection of ninety-nine poems with an allegorical interpretation appended to each. *The Road of Long Study* followed, then her life of Charles V, written at his brother's request. She then returned to her own experience in *The Vision of Christine* which, in spite of a loose allegorical framework, gives us very detailed information about Christine's life. She mentions that between 1399 and 1405 she has written 'fifteen principal volumes, not counting other small ditties, which together fill about fifty quires of large format'. Christine's writing would be stunningly prolific even in an age of typewriters and word-processors; as it is, she has been compared to Lope de Vega for this ability apparently to compose as fast as she could write.

She dedicated copies of her work, often beautifully illuminated, to great ladies and noblemen, who then rewarded her handsomely. Powerful statesmen and distinguished men of letters took an interest in the work of this courageous widow, who was, as a professional woman writer, *sui generis* and moreover had a great many valuable things to say. Her fame spread beyond the borders of France. In 1397 the Earl of Salisbury offered to take her son, Jean, as a page in his household. This arrangement lasted for only two years, however, for Salisbury was executed in 1399 for plotting to kill Henry IV in revenge for the death of Richard II. Henry IV invited Christine to England, but she prudently delayed in giving a direct refusal until her son was safely returned to her. Now Jean entered the service of the Duke of Burgundy. Her other son apparently died in childhood, or at any rate disappeared from the record, and her daughter entered the Dominican convent of St Louis in Poissy, to the west of Paris.

Gian Galeazzo Visconti, Duke of Milan, appealed to Christine's affection for the land of her birth, but the pull of France was stronger. She declined his invitation to ornament the Milanese court with the same firmness with which she had refused Henry IV of England. (And it was just as well, for the Duke of Milan was killed in the Siege of Florence in 1402.)

She had by now collected an impressive list of protectors and admirers in France, including powerful members of the royal family.

Jean, Duke of Berry, collected nearly all of Christine's works in his famous library. Philip the Bold, Duke of Burgundy, commissioned the biography of his brother, Charles V. John the Fearless (Duke of Burgundy after 1404) and Anthony of Burgundy, Duke of Brabant and Limburg, rewarded her for her writing. Both King Charles VI and his queen, Isabeau of Bavaria, gave her generous gifts. (The illumination on the cover of this book is taken from a sumptuous volume Christine once presented to Queen Isabeau and which is now in the British Library.) Louis, Duke of Orleans, and his wife Valentine Visconti (daughter of the Duke of Milan) had a number of Christine's works in their library, as did the Dauphin, Louis de Guyenne and his wife, Marguerite of Burgundy. It was to the latter that Christine dedicated *The Treasure of the City of Ladies*.

With a secure base of patronage, Christine took a leading part in the most celebrated literary controversy of the Middle Ages, the *Querelle*, or debate, of the *Romance of the Rose*. The *Romance of the Rose* was probably the most popular literary work of the Middle Ages, recounting in an immensely long allegory the gradual winning (or seduction) of a lady by her lover. The lady is represented by a prize rose in a garden carefully guarded by such allegorical figures as Danger and Jealousy, often personified as suspicious old crones. The *Romance of the Rose*, begun around 1230 by Guillaume de Lorris, was continued in 1275–80 by Jean de Meung, who introduced a pronounced element of misogyny. Christine, probably one of the few women who had ever read it, attacked its immorality in her *Letter to the God of Love* in 1399. She particularly objected to the generalizations Jean de Meung made about women. She could not understand, she said, why men wrote so scathingly about women when they owed their very existence to them. Had they no gentle feelings for their mothers, sisters, wives, or daughters? Had they never met any virtuous women who might disprove these sweeping generalizations? Had they really passed their lives entirely among immoral women, if indeed they had been acquainted with any women at all? This was fairly radical feminism in a world that held that women were the sources of most sin and the embodiment of both temptation and the deadly sin of lechery. Whether or not Christine was the only woman who had ever read the *Romance of the Rose*, she was certainly the only woman who dared to attack such a universally popular work. She did, however, have three powerful allies in her objections: Jean Gerson, the chancellor of the University of Paris; Guillaume de Tignonville, the provost of

Paris; and Marshal Jean le Meingre Boucicaut. Opposing them were Jean de Montreuil, provost of Lille; Gontier Col, the king's secretary; and his brother Pierre Col, the canon of Paris. The principals in this literary battle circulated some twenty treatises and letters among themselves for the next three years. In the end their disagreement was as strong as ever, but Christine, who had written more than the others put together, had demonstrated her courage in defending what she believed to be right, even in the face of strong opposition.

In 1404 Christine wrote *The Book of the City of Ladies* as her final statement on the issues that had been raised in the controversy over the *Romance of the Rose*. *The Book of the City of Ladies*, alluding to St Augustine's *City of God*, has a loose allegorical structure in which *exempla* about virtuous ladies, borrowed largely from Boccaccio's *De claris mulieribus*, serve as the 'building blocks' for the City, which is to be a haven for all virtuous ladies. The exemplary stories illustrate all the strengths and excellent qualities that the long tradition of misogynist writers claimed that *all* women lacked. With wit and a shrewd appeal to empiricism Christine demolished every argument traditionally put forward to justify the inferior status of women. She demonstrates how a supposed weakness is in fact often a moral strength, as when women, who are physically weak and timid, are therefore more inclined to make peace and avert wars. In a striking passage that must be unique in all medieval literature, Christine advises women to rely on their own experience for knowledge of the feminine condition and not on the ignorant scribbles of men who could not possibly have the same accurate knowledge, no matter what the evidence of their wide reading in the works of other misogynists.

THE TREASURE OF THE CITY OF LADIES

Having put forward her last word on the moral nature of women, Christine went on to write a kind of 'sequel' to *The Book of the City of Ladies*. While *The Treasure of the City of Ladies* (written in 1405, also called *The Book of the Three Virtues*) complements the earlier work in that it is supposed to be the cardinal possession of the ladies now securely sheltered in their allegorical city, it is a book of a very different character. The reader seeking feminist polemics will not find them here. *The Treasure of the City of Ladies* is strictly a guide to practicalities. Part etiquette book, part survival manual, it was written for women who had to live from day to day in the world as it was. The women she addressed ranged from those with power and authority to the poorest peasant women, including widows, spinsters, prostitutes and nuns. This range hardly reflects the real readership that Christine had in mind; rather it reflects a medieval penchant for all-inclusiveness. However, Christine devotes most of her attention to the powerful and well placed. It would be difficult to find more practical social advice in medieval European literature. The society in which great ladies moved was a closed one. The counsel is to be nice to everyone in order to keep a good reputation and also to render the narrow life of the court livable. If a lady is rude or angry to a servant or an equal, she has to live with the friction and hostility she has partly caused. 'Pretend not to notice,' Christine advises, whether it is a husband's infidelity or the jealousy of one's enemies.

Here is advice for making peace between one's husband and his vassals and for keeping the domestic peace with one's spouse and among the ladies of the court. One of her recurring themes is that women should stick together. They should not gossip about each other; they should be tolerant of other women who are much younger or much older than they are; if they are chaste and virtuous they should not assume that other women are not; and they should love each other like sisters. Again and again with casual artistry Christine presents scenes that clearly come straight from life – the great lady waking up in her luxurious bed; the lady positioning herself by her window in the morning so that she can be sure the workmen are all going out to the fields; the lady graciously accepting little gifts from her subjects; the maid pretending that the groceries cost more than they really did; the servants' banquet of purloined food in the kitchen; the women jostling in church, each trying to be the first to the altar. *The Treasure of the City of Ladies* is full of such vivid little pictures of medieval life, startling in their evident authenticity.

Not surprisingly, the only other sources of knowledge we have about medieval chivalry come from the pens of male writers. Modern readers often wonder to what extent the very complicated rules of courtly love actually obtained in the real life of a medieval court. While the lords and ladies were reading fanciful tales of Sir Lancelot and Queen Guinevere, how were they actually behaving towards each other? Christine's allusions to the practice of chivalry in the early fifteenth century are the only reliable picture we possess from the point of view of a woman writing for other women. The message is clear and straight from the shoulder: gallants at court are untrustworthy; they will say anything and make any promise to get their own way. Their promises of secrecy and discretion are worthless; they will brag about their conquest the moment the lady's back is turned. They will badger her for favours and love tokens, but these pleas should be resisted. An adulterous affair is dangerous for everyone concerned, the lady, her husband, her parents and her chaperon (and presumably even for the hectoring and footloose lover, although Christine wastes no sympathy on him). Even in this case, when the popular conventions of courtly flirting can be positively dangerous to a woman with a reputation to protect, Christine does not suggest that the conventions should be changed or abolished: she merely notes that they exist and advises ladies how to deal with them.

Christine assumes that women who do not intend to enter religious orders will marry, although a few may choose to remain in a state of secular virginity, and some will be widowed. Christine's advice concerning widowhood and remarriage comes straight from her own experience. A widow suddenly becomes prey to every sort of swindle and deception. Even men who deferred to her when her husband was alive are now rude and dismissive. People will bring lawsuits against her, and she herself may be forced to go to law to obtain justice. After her husband's death people will try to cheat her out of what is rightfully hers. If you cannot settle it amicably out of court, Christine counsels from bitter experience, get a *good* lawyer, an old one who knows all the tricks, but be careful that the legal fees do not exceed the sum you stand to gain by litigation!

In view of all the problems of widowhood, Christine might be expected to advise remarriage, but she does not. She presents this argument, but reminds her readers that marriage is not always better than independence, even of this difficult and penurious sort:

If in married life everything were all repose and peace, truly it would be sensible for a woman to enter it again, but because one sees quite the contrary, any woman ought to be very wary of remarriage, although for young women it may be a necessity or anyway very convenient. But for those who have already passed their youth and who are well enough off and are not constrained by poverty, it is sheer folly, although some women who wish to remarry say that it is no life for a woman on her own. So few widows trust in their own intelligence that they excuse themselves by saying that they would not know how to look after themselves.

Ladies, whether married or widowed, living on country estates should know how the estate is administered and run. The country lady should also know the details of crop management and animal husbandry so that she can oversee her workmen intelligently. Any woman with a household to run should know how to budget the money. Christine gives practical instructions for allocating income and staying out of debt: divide your expenditure into five categories of descending priorities; give to the poor, pay your debts and household expenses, pay your servants and staff, put something aside for gifts, and save the remainder to spend on your own clothing and jewellery.

One of Christine's overriding concerns – a concern that is evident in much of her advice – is for peace. A princess or great lady should try to make peace between her husband and any rebellious vassals or subjects. A lady should keep peace in her family and among the ladies and women of her household. Men are a little inclined to be hot-headed, she says, and it is a woman's duty to bring a measure of calmness and reason to a hostile situation. A lady should establish herself as a mediator between any hostile factions, whether it is a question of national politics or friction in the household. The queen or princess can become the power behind the throne by exerting her calming influence. Women generally should work behind the scenes, tactfully, even stealthily, on a personal level. The wife, at whatever level of society, must defer to her husband. In the absence of her husband, however, the wife should act as his representative, whether she is a queen presiding over his council or an artisan's wife overseeing her husband's subordinates.

CHRISTINE'S LATER WORKS

When Christine de Pisan finished writing *The Treasure of the City of Ladies* she was forty and could look back on a distinguished career in letters. She had written nineteen or twenty major works in both poetry and prose. To these she added *The Body of Policy*, about the instruction of princes, written with the young Dauphin in mind, as a companion piece to *The Treasure of the City of Ladies*.

The peaceful atmosphere in Paris quickly deteriorated after 1407, when Louis, Duke of Orleans, was assassinated by the Burgundian faction. Christine stayed on in Paris until 1418, when she finally escaped the civil war by entering a convent. In the meantime she continued to write. In *The Book of Feats of Arms and of Chivalry* she compiles the wisdom of several classical authors and adds her own judgements and observations, including practical information she has gleaned from soldiers with battle experience. Always concerned with very practical, usable advice, Christine describes how to choose a camp-ground, what food and bedding a general will need for a campaign, how to attack a stronghold, and conversely, how to prevent the undermining of one's own castle. Such was the usefulness of this handbook that eighty years later Henry VII asked William Caxton to translate it into English and print it for the benefit of English men-at-arms.

Although the licentious and disorganized court of Queen Isabeau inspired Christine to write some of her works about good government and well-run courts, she seems to have followed her own advice and kept on the good side of the queen. Soon after Christine finished *The Treasure of the City of Ladies*, the queen asked her for a collection of her complete works to date. Although all of the love poems are included, the biography of Charles V and the just completed *Treasure* are omitted, the latter being perhaps a little too close to home for the queen's taste. There are a number of new poems in this collection, and no doubt Queen Isabeau was considerably more interested in poems about ladies and knights, separated lovers and bittersweet re-unions, than in moral instruction about the proper management of a hypothetical court that greatly resembled her own.

Christine de Pisan was now reasonably well off financially, thanks to her prolific composition and her influential patronage, and she was well known both at home and abroad. In 1409 she wrote *Seven Allegorical Psalms* at the request of Charles the Noble, King of Navarre. They include some workmanlike prayers, composed as an exercise in a genre by special request. But in the summer of the next year she wrote something very much nearer her own taste for debate on public affairs. France was about to be torn apart by civil war, and Christine, ever the French patriot and seeker of reconciliation, wrote an open letter to those in power called *Lamentation on the Evils of Civil War*. She describes the death and ruin that would result from civil war. She begs the powers that be to avert the impending national catastrophe. She signs her letter 'A poor voice crying in this kingdom, desirous of peace and the good of all of you, your servant Christine, who prays that she may see the day when peace comes.' But 23 August 1410, the date of the letter, was too late to have much effect on the growing dissension among the factions in the realm. After the hostilities had gone on for another two years and a shaky treaty was concluded, Christine exultantly addressed her *Book of Peace* to the Dauphin. After having lauded Charles V in *The Book of the Deeds and Good Customs of Charles V* (1404) and, in the *Body of Policy* (written in 1406 or 1407), explained in detail how a ruler should be educated, Christine now seeks to instil all the princely virtues into the adolescent Dauphin before it is too late. *The Book of Peace* was finished by the end of 1413. (Christine always presented a copy of her latest work to Jean, Duke of Berry, as a New Year's present, and as a result we have good evidence of the order in which she wrote her works and her speed of composition. *The Book of Peace*, Christine's last major work, was presented to the Duke of Berry on the first day of 1414.)

Ten years before Agincourt, Christine had warned that if civil war broke out, France would lay itself open to attack by a foreign power. When the old Duke of Berry died in the following year (1416), all of Christine's friends from the great days of Charles V were either dead or prisoners of war. Fortune's wheel had dipped yet again. She wrote one last work before entering her convent: the *Letter of the Prison of Human Life*, addressed to Marie of Berry to help console her for the death or imprisonment of several members of her family. In 1418, not long before the Burgundians seized control of Paris, Christine retired to the safety of a convent, perhaps the one at Poissy where her daughter was a nun. Unable to leave her literary work entirely, Christine wrote some short prayers for the consolation of bereaved women, but for most of her time at the convent – from 1418 until her death some time after 1429 – we have no evidence that she wrote anything else, except her final work, which must have been written shortly before her death.

The *Hymn to Joan of Arc*, although a minor work compared to Christine's other books, should have been enough by itself to ensure Christine's fame, because it is the only contemporary tribute to Joan of Arc and the only evidence of her achievements outside the trial records written during her lifetime. Christine was enthusiastic about Joan of Arc, as she exemplified both the heroism of women and the victory of good over evil in French politics. The main concerns of Christine's life seemed to come together at last: good government, the dignity of women, and domestic and international peacemaking and justice.

Christine's date and place of death are unknown. She may or may not have lived to see the fall of Joan of Arc. The convent at Poissy is now in ruins and its records destroyed. All that remains of Christine de Pisan are the volumes that her lively mind produced and the portraits that illustrate some of them. Many of them have never been edited for the modern reader and most of them have never been translated. Christine has never been irretrievably lost, however. Her writings have been misplaced, discovered, rediscovered and attributed to other people, but in the end she will take her place with the great writers of the Middle Ages.

THE TREASURE
OF THE CITY OF LADIES

PROLOGUE

After I built the City of Ladies with the help and by the commandment of the three Ladies of Virtue, Reason, Rectitude and Justice, in the form and manner explained in the text of that book, and after I, more than anyone else, had worked so hard to finish the project and felt so exhausted by the long and continual exertion, I wanted only to rest and be idle for a while. But those same three ladies appeared to me again, and all three lost no time in saying the same kind of thing to me: 'What, my studious daughter, have you already put away the tool of your intelligence and consigned it to silence? Have you let your ink dry and abandoned your pen and the labour of your right hand, when you used to take such pleasure in it? Do you now intend to take seriously the propaganda of Laziness, who, if you are inclined to believe it, will sing sweetly to you: "You have done enough. It is time that you had a rest."

'But don't you know that, although after great labour the wise person rests his mind, now is not the time to abandon good work? It is not like you to be among those who give up in mid-course. The knight who leaves the field of battle before the moment of victory is deeply shamed, for the laurel wreath belongs to those who persevere. Now stand up and make your hand ready; get up out of the ashes of indolence!

'Hear our lectures and you will accomplish good work. We do not want to overwork you, but we have considered our virtuous labours, discussed them, and made a decision with the counsel of virtues and the example of God, who in the beginning of the world that He had created saw that His work was good and He blessed it. Then He made man and woman and the animals. Similarly may that preceding work of ours, the *City of Ladies*, which is good and useful, be blessed and exalted throughout the entire world so that this same work may be further disseminated.

'We hope that just as the wise birdcatcher readies his cage before he may take his birds, so, after the shelter of honoured ladies is made and prepared, devices and traps may be set with your help as before. You will spread fine and noble nets and snares that we will provide you throughout the land in the places and localities and in all the corners where ladies and generally all women pass and congregate, so that those who are wild and hard to tame can be grabbed, taken and snared in our nets so that no one or very few who get caught can escape and all or the largest part of them may be installed in the cage of our glorious city, where they may take up the sweet song of those who are already sheltered there as sovereign ladies and who unceasingly sing hosannas in harmony with the blessed angels.'

Then I, Christine, hearing the soft voices of my very reverend mentors, filled with joy and trembling, immediately roused myself and knelt before them and offered myself in obedience to their noble wishes. Then I received from them this command: 'Take your pen and write. Blessed will they be who live in our city to swell the number of citizens of virtue. May all the feminine college and their devout community be apprised of the sermons and lessons of wisdom. First of all to the queens, princesses and great ladies, and then on down the social scale we will chant our doctrine to the other ladies and maidens and all classes of women, so that the syllabus of our school may be valuable to all.' Amen.

Part One

I. This is the beginning of the book that Dame Christine de Pisan made for all great queens, ladies and princesses. And first, how they ought to love and fear God.

From us three sisters, daughters of God, named Reason, Rectitude and Justice, to all princesses, empresses, queens, duchesses and high-born ladies ruling over the Christian world, and generally to all women: loving greetings.

Be it known that as charitable love prompts us to desire the well-being and spiritual development, the honour and prosperity of all women, and to wish the downfall and destruction of everything that could prevent them, we feel moved to address some words of instruction to you. Come, therefore, everyone, to the school of wisdom. Ladies raised to high estate, in spite of your greatness do not be ashamed to humble yourselves enough to hear our lessons, for, according to the word of God, whosoever humbles himself will be raised up. What in this world is more pleasant or more delectable to those who desire worldly riches than gold and precious stones? But yet those riches cannot enhance an ambitious person as much as virtues do, for virtues are nobler, because they endure forever and are the treasures of the soul, which is everlasting, while the others pass away like smoke, and so those who have tasted them desire them all the more ardently, more than any other earthly thing can be desired. Therefore it is fitting that those men and women who are placed by grace and good fortune in the highest estates should be provided with the very best things. And since virtues are the food of our table, we are pleased to distribute them first to those ladies to whom we speak, that is, to the above-mentioned princesses, and this will be the foundation of our teaching: first of all the love of and the fear of Our Lord, for this is the cardinal principle of wisdom, from which all the other virtues spring.

Therefore listen, princesses and ladies honoured on earth, how first of all above all else you must love and fear Our Lord. Why love Him? For His infinite goodness and for the very great blessings that you receive from Him. Fear Him for His divine and holy justice, which leaves nothing unpunished. If you have this love and fear constantly

35

in view, you will infallibly be on the way to the goal where our instruction will lead you, that is, to the virtues. Now this is true, and there is no doubt that all hearts that love well should show it by good works, as He Himself says in the Gospel: 'My father's lambs love me and I watch over them.' That is, the creatures who love Him follow in His footsteps, which are virtuous, and He keeps them from all dangers. This is the way that the princess who loves Him shows it, for whatever duties or occupations she has due to the magnificence of her position, she will always keep before her eyes the light of the straight and narrow path. This light will combat temptations and the shadows of sin and vices and will conquer them and dispel them in the manner contained in what follows.

2. How temptations can come to a high-born princess.

When the princess or high-born lady wakes up in the morning, she sees herself lying luxuriously in her bed between soft sheets, surrounded by rich accoutrements and everything for bodily comfort, and ladies-in-waiting around her focusing all their attention on her and seeing that she lacks for nothing, ready to run to her if she gives the least sigh or if she breathes a word, their knees flexed to administer any service to her and to obey all her commands. And so it often happens that temptation will assail her, singing sweetly: 'By Almighty God, is there in this world a greater lady than you or one with more authority? To whom should you defer, for don't you take precedence over everyone else? This or that woman, even if she is married to a great prince, cannot be compared to you. You are richer, or have a better lineage, or are more respected because of your children, more feared, and more renowned and wield more authority because of your husband's power. Therefore who would dare to displease you in any way? Would you not well and truly avenge yourself with such power and such other advantages?

'Therefore there is no one so great that you do not have power over him. Any time such and such a man or woman is arrogant towards you and presumptuously intends to harm you and does such and such a thing to cause your displeasure, you can avenge yourself later when you see your chance, and you will be able to do it very well with the power you have.'

But what good does it do you to do that?

36

'No one accomplishes anything, however skilled he may be, nor is anyone feared if he has no money or considerable financial resources. If you can manage to amass treasure so that you can look after your own needs, it is the surest course and the best friend you can have. Who would dare to disobey you, seeing that you have great resources to dispense? If you pay only low wages, your servants will still serve you gladly in the hope of eventually getting more money, for your wealth will be well known. You will have no trouble with this, and if there is any talk about it, such gossip cannot hurt you. What should you care? All you have to worry about is pleasing yourself. You have only your leisurely life in this world – what else can you need? You cannot lack for wines and foods; you can have them whenever you like, and every other pleasure. In brief, you need not bother about anything else except having all the delight and all the amusement that you can in this world. No one has a good time if he does not provide it for himself. You must have a carefree heart to make you happy and to give you a merry life. You must have such gowns, such ornaments, such jewels and such clothing made in a particular way and of a particular cut. It's no more than you deserve.'

3. How the good princess who loves and fears Our Lord can resist temptations by means of divine inspiration.

All the above-mentioned things or similar ones are the dishes that Temptation sets before everyone who lives a life of ease and pleasure. But what will the good princess do when she feels herself tempted in this way? Then she will need the unshakeable love and fear of Our Lord God Jesus Christ, who will teach her some home truths, speaking like this: 'O foolish and ill-advised simpleton, what can you be thinking of? Have you forgotten what you really are? Don't you realize that you are a poor and miserable creature, frail, weak, and subject to all infirmities, passions, diseases and other pains that a mortal body can suffer? What advantage do you have over anyone else? What advantage would a pile of earth covered by finery have over one that was under a poor rag? O pitiful creature given to sin and every vice, do you want then, in that case, to ignore your true essence and forget how this wretched vessel empty of any virtue, that desires honours and comforts so much, will break and die shortly? It will be food for the worms and will rot in the earth as much as the poorest woman there

37

is, and the unhappy soul will take with it nothing except the good or evil that the wretched body has done on earth. What will honours be worth to you then, or possessions or your family, which you boast of so much in this world? Will they help you in the torments you will endure if you have lived wickedly in this world? Certainly not, but rather everything that you have abused will lead you to ruin. Alas, pitiful woman, it would have been better for you to have lived a troubled life as a poor woman than to be elevated to such great rank, which will be (if you are not on your guard against it) the cause of your damnation. For it is difficult to be among the flames without getting burned.

'Don't you know what God says in the Gospel, that the poor are blessed and that theirs is the kingdom of heaven? And elsewhere He says that a rich man can no more enter paradise than a laden camel can go through the eye of a needle.

'O pitiful woman, you are so blinded that you do not perceive your great peril. The cause of it is great pride, which, because of the vain honours that surround you, overrides all reason in you, so that you do not imagine yourself to be only a princess or a great lady, but like a veritable goddess in this world. Oh, this false pride! How can you tolerate it in yourself? You know very well, from the report of the Scriptures, that God hates it so much that He cannot endure it, for because of this He exiled Lucifer, the prince of devils, from Heaven into Hell, and He will undoubtedly do the same to you if you are not careful.'

'O Pride, root of all evil, certainly I know that from you spring all the other vices, and I can recognize this in myself, for because of you and not for any other reason I often fly into a rage, desiring vengeance, as I recently did. Pride makes me imagine that I ought to be feared and esteemed above all others, and that I ought always to have my own way, and for this reason I ought not to put up with anything that displeases me, but immediately avenge myself, however small the insult might be. O perilous vanity, bloated wilfulness, carbuncle full of poison and putrefaction, the flesh that harbours you is at greater risk than that which contains a plague bubo.

'Perverse creature, you desire vengeance because it seems to you that you are so great that, whatever you do, no one ought to dare to contradict or object to your wishes, but your blind ignorance, egged on by proud arrogance, makes you fail to realize how any person, be he great or little, who passes his days in wickedness deserves all

38

his wishes to be opposed. If you do not reflect on what you have deserved and now deserve because of your behaviour, you will not be in favour with very many people. For this reason it is not without cause that several women rebel against you and contradict your wishes and opinions, and thus you do not consider your offence, but at every turn you imagine that everything that you do can overrule all other wills and opinions. And if any people resist or contradict it, you hate them and plot against them and secretly or openly persecute them, without considering the evil and the very great peril which can result from it for you yourself and an infinite number of others, in body and soul. Or if you do not persecute them because you cannot, at least you harbour mortal hatred for them. This treacherous pride that maroons you in the sea of perdition – does it also put into your head (because of vanity or the desire to achieve either your revenge or other useless things) the idea of amassing treasures without regard to conscience? O, painful Treasure! It is nearly impossible for you to be amassed without harm to many people. And against their wishes they yield wickedly to your own desire.'

Know for certain, and do not doubt it, that you will never use with much joy the wealth you have acquired and amassed unfairly, for just when you have assembled it with the intention of using it in some way at your pleasure, God will send you so much adversity or affliction or other burdens that this damnable treasure will turn out to be disagreeable and painful to use, quite contrary to what you intend. What will you do then with this treasure? Will you take it with you when you die? Certainly not, but only the burden of what you have wickedly acquired and used. But look again where this cursed pride puts you. Because it makes you believe that you surpass everyone else in grandeur and authority, it makes your heart quite sad and fearful that someone else may be able to overtake you and reach your high estate. Because it makes you always wish to be greater, if it happens that you see or learn about someone with as much or more authority or honour than you, no pain could be greater than the sorrow that your heart carries. This pain makes you spiteful, wrathful and malicious.

A second little flame from Hell makes you proud. You say to yourself, 'It's not your duty, place or trade to labour or to work at anything. You have nothing to do but to see to your own comforts, to sleep late in the morning, and then after dinner to rest, inspect your chests of jewels and ornaments – this is your rightful employment.' And so, unhappy witless creature that you are, does it seem to you that God, who has given time to each person to put to good use, has given you, more than another, the authority to spend it in lazy idleness? O wretched creature, you have heard it preached before that St Bernard says of the Canticles that Idleness is the mother of all error and the wicked stepmother of the virtues. Idleness makes even a strong and constant man stumble into sin, which destroys all the virtues, nourishes Pride and builds the road to Hell. But what else comes of this Pride? This Pride, which thus makes you love your comforts, and those comforts, which nourish that Pride so much, make you desire voluptuous pleasures in eating and drinking, and by no means common things nor customary food, for you are quite tired of them. The cooks, to please you and to earn their wages, have to devise seasonings, garnishes and new sauces to make the meat more pleasant to your taste. Likewise, you demand the finest wines.

O sorrowful woman, is it necessary thus to fill up this belly which is, after all, only food for worms and the vessel of all wickedness? But what happens to it when it is thus filled? What does it ask, just like the mouth, but the nourishment of passion, luxury, and voluptuousness, and excess of wines and of meats and the nourishment of carnality? This is what inflames Pride and predisposes the will to desire in all ways everything that can delight the body. Flesh thus nourished resembles the horse which, when its master tries hard to spur it on, is so strong and skittish that when he thinks to ride it he cannot control it. It bolts with him in spite of the roads being hazardous, and finally through its resistance and wrongheadedness it breaks the rider's neck. In exactly this way the body too much overfed and excited by voluptuous foods kills the soul and the virtues, but Pride, which flourishes on this rich food, makes you so much desire extravagant clothing, jewels and finery that you hardly think of anything else, neither what they must have cost nor where they must have come from, nor how you may have acquired them. Besides leading you to other unseemly, disreputable and boundless vices, Pride makes you so disdainful and aloof to serve that one can hardly find jewels, clothing or ornaments that are good enough for you. In addition to all these things, you are so impertinent and presumptuous that it seems to you that neither God Himself nor anything else can impose upon you.

O miserable, wretched and blind creature! How can this outrageous pride have so much power over you that it makes you forget the punishments of God, even though He allows you to stay immersed for so long in so many faults without paying you your just deserts? Do you not know that a holy doctor of the Church says that the slower the vengeance of God is in coming, the more perilous it is when it does come? Likewise, the more the bow is bent, the more piercing is the arrow when it comes. Have you forgotten how Our Lord punished for his pride Nebuchadnezzar, who was king of Babylon and so great a prince that he feared no one? Similarly the great king of Persia, Antiochus, was punished, and also the Emperor Xerxes and a great number of others who were so great and powerful that there was nothing in Heaven or earth that they feared. And always by the vengeance and will of God they were so humbled and reduced to such confusion for their punishment that there was no man born in the world who was more miserable or more unfortunate than they became.

Do you not remember in connection with this that it is written in the Book of Ecclesiasticus in the tenth chapter, as you have heard your confessor relate, that God has cast down the thrones of proud princes and has set up the meek in their stead, and has plucked up the roots of the proud nations and has planted the lowly in their place? This means nothing else than that He destroys the proud and exalts the humble. So you are doing the right thing if you want to be destroyed!

By Almighty God, you who are a simple little woman who has no strength, power or authority unless it is conferred on you by someone else, do you imagine that you are surrounded by luxury and honour so that you can dominate and outdo the whole world at your will?

4. The good and holy reason and knowledge that comes to the good princess through the love and fear of Our Lord.

Thus the good princess, admonished by God, who loves and fears Our Lord, will come to her senses. However good she is, she will say to herself: 'Now you see and recognize by the grace of Almighty God the terrifying perils in which you have put yourself all because of this damnable pride! What are you going to do about it? Has it become such a habit? Do you want to be damned? Which is worth more to you: to live in this world for a little while at your ease and be damned perpetually (but not really at your ease, because the more you involve yourself in the delights of the world and the more you remember various desires – which will torment your heart, because you cannot fulfil them or gain your wishes – the more your heart will never be content), or to refrain from your extravagant pleasures and live in the love and fear of Our Lord and be saved in the Kingdom without end?

'Alas, damned woman – and what is it to be damned? Holy Scripture says that it is to be deprived always and eternally of the sight of God and to be in terrifying darkness in the company of horrible devils, the enemies of human beings. The souls of the damned wail terrible lamentations, cursing God and their parents and themselves in unimaginable torment in burning fire. In short, it is to be in indescribable fear and in perpetual horror, and furthermore, what makes it even worse is the hopelessness of ever escaping from it.

'Oh poor woman, do you want to sink into such damnation and lose by your folly the grace that God promises you if you try to deserve it by only a little effort? And what does He promise you? He has promised you by virtue of His holy passion that if you choose to keep His commandments, you will go to Paradise. St Gregory, speaking in his homilies of this city of Paradise, says, in brief, "Where is the tongue and the understanding that can comprehend or say what or how great are the joys of Paradise, to be always in the company of angels with the blessed saints in the glory of our Creator, to see the glorious visage of God and the Holy Trinity face to face, to see and look at and feel His incomprehensible light, to be relieved of all desires, to have knowledge of all learning, to be in eternal rest, never to be afraid of death, and to be assured of remaining in this blessed glory forever?"

'Now you see the difference between the two paths. Which one will you take? Will you mire yourself down, in danger of suffocation, and leave the clean, beautiful and safe way which leads to salvation? No, no, you will not be so foolish as to lay aside the good in order to take up the evil!

'O Holy Trinity, one God in unity, sovereign power, perfect wisdom, and infinite goodness, counsel me and help me to escape the shadows of ignorance that have so dimmed my sight. Pure and holy Virgin, comfort of the grief-stricken, hope of true believers, hold my hand in your holy mercy, and rescue me from the slough of sin and iniquity. Most holy and blessed company of the court of Paradise, angels and archangels, cherubim and seraphim, thrones and dominions, saints, apostles of God, martyrs, virgins and celibates, pray for me and be my help.'

5. Of the two holy lives, namely the active life and the contemplative life.

Now, therefore, here is what you have to do if you wish to be saved. Scripture mentions two paths that lead to Heaven, and without following one or the other of these paths it is impossible to enter it. One is called the contemplative life and the other the active life. But what exactly are the contemplative life and the active life?

The contemplative life is a manner and condition of serving God in which a person so ardently desires Our Lord that she entirely forgets everyone else – father, mother, children, and even herself – for a very great and passionate concentration on her Creator. She constantly thinks of Him and Him alone. All other things are nothing to her, nor does she experience poverty, tribulation or other torment with which any other creature might be afflicted. These afflictions could be an obstacle to the upright contemplative heart, but it pays no attention to them. Her approach to life is to scorn utterly everything that is of the world and its pleasures. Her object is to keep herself solitary and withdrawn from human society, on bended knee, her hands joined together, her eyes looking to Heaven, her heart exalted by high thoughts. She goes before God to contemplate and consider by holy inspiration the blessed Trinity, the heavenly host and the joys of Heaven. In this condition the perfect contemplative is often so ecstatic that she does not seem to be herself. The consolation, peacefulness and joy that she then feels cannot be described, neither can any other joy be compared to that one, for she is tasting the glories and joys of Paradise – that is, she sees God in spirit through contemplation. She burns in her love and has perfect contentment in this world, for she neither wishes nor desires anything else, and God comforts her, for she is His servant. He sets before her fragrant dishes from His holy Paradise; they are pure and holy thoughts which come from Heaven and give confident hope of joining that happy company. There is truly no joy like it. Those who know it have tried to describe it. I regret that I can only talk about it in this indirect way, as a blind person might discourse upon colours. That this life is more agreeable to God than any other has often been made clear to the world. It has been

43

demonstrated and written by various men and women contemplative saints who have been seen in their contemplation raised above the earth by a miracle of God, as though the body wished to follow the thoughts that had mounted to Heaven. Of this holy and most exalted life I am not worthy to speak nor to describe it as it deserves, but there are many sacred writings that describe this fully, and so my attempt would be unnecessary anyway.

The active life is another way of serving God. The active life means that the person who wishes to follow it will be so charitable that, if she could, she would render service to everyone for the love of God. She goes around to the hospitals, visits the sick and the poor, according to her ability, helps them at her own expense and physical effort for the love of God. She has such great pity for people she sees in sin or misery that she weeps for them as though their distress were her own. She loves her neighbour's welfare as much as her own, is always striving to do good, is never idle; her heart burns ceaselessly with desire to do works of mercy, to which she devotes herself with all her might. Such a woman bears all injuries and tribulations patiently for the love of God.

As you can see, this active life has more use in the world than the other one. These are both of great excellence, but Our Lord Jesus Christ himself judged the greater excellence of the two, when Mary Magdalene*, who represents the contemplative life, was seated at the feet of Our Lord as one who had no thought for anything else and who utterly burned with her holy love. And Mary Martha, her sister, by whom is understood the active life, was the hostess of Our Lord. She worked in the house in the service of Jesus and his Apostles and complained that Mary her sister did not help her. But Our Lord excused her, saying, 'Martha, you are very diligent, and your work is good and necessary, but Mary has chosen the better part.' By this 'part' that she had chosen it can be understood that, although the active life is of great excellence and necessary for the help and succour of many, contemplation, which is to give up the world and all its cares to think only of Him, is the greatest and worthiest perfection. For this reason holy men have in the past established religious orders. In God's eyes life in a religious community is the highest level of life there is. Anyone who founds a religious order so that those who wish to live in

*Christine has confused Mary Magdalene with Mary the sister of Martha (Luke 10:38–42).

44

contemplation can be separated there from the world in the service of God without any other cares pleases not only those people, but also God, who would be pleased indeed that each one said his offices there.

6. The life that the good princess decides to lead.

The good princess who has been inspired by God says to herself, 'You must decide which of these paths you wish to take. It is commonly said, and it is true, that Discretion is the mother of the virtues. And why is she the mother? Because she guides and sustains the others, and anyone who fails to do any undertaking through her will find that all the work comes to nothing and is of no effect, because it is necessary to work by Discretion. This is what I must consider before I undertake anything at all.

'First I ought to think of the strength or weakness of my poor body and the frailty to which I am inclined, and also of what level of submission it is appropriate for me to assume, according to the estate where God has called me and which He has entrusted to me in this world. If I consider these things honestly, I will find that although I have some good intentions, I am too weak to suffer great abstinence and great pain, and my spirit is weak through frailty and inconstancy. And since I feel myself to be like that, I should not imagine that I am more virtuous than I am, even though God says, "You must forsake father and mother for my name." I'm afraid that I would not be at all able to fulfil my pledge and leave husband, children, everyday life, and all worldly concerns with the hope of serving only God, as women of the greatest perfection have done. Therefore I should not attempt something I wouldn't be able to persevere with. What shall I do then? Choose the active life? Alas, happy are those who succeed in the work they have been commanded to perform. O God, as You have established me in the world as a mere woman, I can at least serve You perfectly in ministering and doing service to Your "members", that is, the poor, for love of You. Alas, how would I ever manage to abandon all worldly position? Although I know very well that there is nothing else I love and desire except only You, and that all pleasure is nothing, I do not have the strength in myself to be able to abandon every worldly thing. I am very frightened about what to do, for You say that it is impossible for the rich to be saved.'

45

At this juncture Holy Inspiration comes to the good princess and speaks to her in this manner:

'Now here is what you must do. God does not command anyone to leave everything to follow Him; that is only for those who wish to pursue the very most ideal life. Each person can be saved in his own station in life, and when God says it is impossible for a rich person to be saved, that means a person who has riches without virtues and who does not distribute his riches in alms and good deeds, a person whose whole happiness is in possessing great wealth. There is no doubt that God hates such people and that they will never enter the Kingdom of Heaven unless they change their ways. And as for the poor, who He says are blessed, those are the poor in spirit. Even a very rich and wealthy man could be poor in spirit if he does not prize the riches of the world, and if he has any of them, he distributes them in good works and in the service of God, and if he neither prides himself on his honour nor thinks himself greater because of his wealth. Such a person, even though he is wealthy in worldly goods, is poor of spirit and will possess the Kingdom of Heaven, and you can see the evidence of it. Have there not been a great host of kings and princes who are saints in Paradise, like St Louis, King of France, and several others who did not retire from the world but reigned and possessed their lordships at the pleasure of God? They lived justly, but not because they did not appreciate glory or rejected the honours that they were given. They considered that honour belonged not to their own persons, but to the status of their power and wealth, of which they were vicars of God on earth. Similarly there are a great many queens and princesses who are saints in Paradise, like the wife of King Clovis of France and St Badour and St Elizabeth, Queen of Hungary, and many others. There is no doubt at all that God wishes to be served by people of all conditions. At every level of society anyone who wants to can be saved, for the rank does not cause damnation, but rather not knowing how to use it wisely.'

Therefore in conclusion, the princess says to herself, 'I see very well that, as I do not feel myself to be the sort of person who can whole-heartedly choose and follow one of these two lives, I will try hard at least to strike a happy medium, as St Paul counsels, and take as much as I can from both lives according to my ability.'

7. How the good princess will wish to cultivate all virtues.

The good princess will have these or similar ideas by divine inspiration, and in order to put them into effect, she will see that she needs to be well informed by good and wise people about what is right and what is wrong, so that she can choose the one and avoid the other. Although every mortal person is by nature given to sin, to the best of her ability she will avoid mortal sin especially, and will try to follow the example of a good physician who cures a disease by its opposite. She will follow the words of Chrysostom on the Gospel of St Matthew, who says, 'Whoever wishes to have riches in Heaven should cultivate earthly humility, for in the eyes of God the one who is most grand and elevated in honours here below is not the greatest, but the one who is most just on earth is the greatest in Heaven.' And because the good princess will know that honours usually increase pride, her heart will be altogether inclined towards humility. She will think that although it is appropriate to the rank of her husband and of her class that she should receive honours, she will control her heart and it will not be wounded with arrogance nor puffed up with pride, but she will render thanks to God and attribute all honour to Him. She will always recognize in her heart that she is a poor mortal creature, frail and sinful, and that the rank that she receives is only an office for which she will soon have to account to God, for her life in comparison to the life everlasting is only a short time. This noble princess, therefore, although the dignity of her rank requires that she receive great reverence from people, will not take any personal delight in it when it is paid her. At the very least, she should preserve the honour of her position. She will behave respectably and speak softly; her conduct will be kindly and her expression gentle and pleasant, greeting everyone with lowered eyes. She will greet people in words so humane and so sweet that they may be agreeable both to God and to the world.

Besides this virtue of humility, the noble lady will wish to be so patient that although the world delivers a good deal of adversity to great lords and ladies as well as to humble persons, she will not be impatient, regardless of what comes to her. She will take all adversity willingly for the love of Our Lord and will give thanks to Him for it with a good heart. Indeed, she will be so much disposed towards this virtue of patience, that if it should happen that she receives some wrong or sorrow from some person or group of people (as often happens to many ladies without cause), she will not seek, nor wish, nor try

47

to obtain their punishment. If it happens that they are punished by law and by justice, she will have pity on them, remembering that God commanded us to love our enemies and that St Paul says that charity does not seek even what is its own; she will pray to God for them that He may have mercy on them and give them patience.

This noble lady, so disposed by great steadfastness and strength of courage, will not take much notice of the darts of the envious. That is, if she finds out that some words have been said against her, as happens every day to the best of ladies, she will nevertheless not be perturbed about it nor will she regard it as a great crime, but will pardon it easily. Nor will she ever for her high rank bear a grudge against anyone who has done her a great injury, being mindful of the great injuries that Our Lord suffered for us, and yet He prayed for those who tormented Him. The excellent lady will suspect that in some way she may have deserved it, and so virtue will provide her with the teaching of Seneca, who says, speaking of princes and princesses or powerful persons, that it is a very great merit in God's eyes, praiseworthy to the world, and a sign of noble virtue to dismiss easily the wrong that one might easily avenge, and it sets a good example to the common people. St Gregory asserts this same thing in the twenty-second book of *Morals*, where he says that no one is perfect if he has not patience in the face of the evils that his neighbours do him. For whoever does not bear patiently the wrongdoing of another is impatient and proves that he is far from the fullness of virtues. In praising patience St Gregory says that just as the rose flowers sweetly and is beautiful among the sharp thorns, the patient person is also victoriously resplendent among those who strive to harm him.

This princess who would strive to amass virtue upon virtue will remember that St Paul says that if someone has all other virtues and continually worships, goes on pilgrimages, makes great fasts and great abstinences and does all the good that he can and yet does not have charity in himself, all this will profit him nothing. And for this reason she, ever mindful of this teaching, will wish to have this excellent virtue so that she will be so compassionate towards all people that the wrongdoing of another will pain her like her own. Her charity will make her not only feel sorrow when she sees people in affliction, but oblige her to roll up her sleeves and help them as much as she can. And as a wise doctor of the Church says, charity exists in many modes and is not to be understood as helping another person only with money from your purse, but also with help and comfort by your speech and advice wherever the need arises and with all the good that you can do.

And so this lady will be, by pure, mild and holy charity, an advocate and mediator between the prince her husband (or her child if she is a widow) and her people, or all people whom she may be able to help by doing good, depending on the situation. Sometimes it may happen that the prince, by bad counsel or from some other cause, will try to oppress his people with some expense. The subjects will realize that their lady is full of pity, goodness and charity, and will come to her and very humbly beseech her to represent them to the prince, for they are very poor and would not be able to meet such an expense without very great hardship or without being ruined. If they have offended the prince, whether because of someone's gossip or flattery or because they deserve his displeasure, they will come humbly to her to beg her to make peace for them. Or if they wish to ask some favour or privilege, the good princess will never refuse to speak to them, nor will she make a great show of keeping them waiting. Receiving them very kindly, she will listen patiently and be attentive to everything they have to say. She will be accompanied by wise and upright gentlemen who will counsel her. She will reply wisely and suitably with the help of the good advice of those men; she will excuse her husband and speak well of him. If for any reason her subjects feel disgruntled with her reply, she will say that she promises to try her best to make peace, or to stand as their good friend in the petition they are making and in everything else in her power. She will ask them always to be loyal, good and obedient towards their lord, and in return they can always rely on her for help in emergencies, for she will not fail them in anything she can do.

In this way the noble lady will reply so wisely to the ambassadors of the people or of her subjects that when they go away from her they will be satisfied to the extent that if they previously had some grievance, rebellion or quarrel in mind, they will all be pacified. The good lady will not make them waste their time in vain hope, but without long delay she will scrupulously keep her word about what she has promised them; she will speak to her husband well and wisely, calling in other wise persons if necessary, and will very humbly petition him on behalf of the people. She will show the reasons, which she will understand thoroughly, and she will show how it is necessary for a prince, if he wishes to reign long in peace and glory, to be loved by his subjects and by his people. She will address him according to the form that Seneca lays down in the third book of *De Ira*, which says that although it may be good for everyone to practise kindness, it is especially advisable for the prince to exercise it towards his subjects. And so, in brief, she will make such an effort and pursue the thing so thoroughly that she will have all or part of her request, and so sensibly will she report it to the subjects that they will feel satisfied with the prince and with her, and they will thank her most humbly.

8. How the good and wise princess will make every effort to restore peace between the prince and the barons if there is any discord.

If any neighbouring or foreign prince wishes for any reason to make war against her husband, or if her husband wishes to make war on someone else, the good lady will consider this thing carefully, bearing in mind the great evils and infinite cruelties, destruction, massacres and detriment to the country that result from war; the outcome is often terrible. She will ponder long and hard whether she can do something (always preserving the honour of her husband) to prevent this war. In this cause she will wish to work and labour carefully, calling God to her aid, and by good counsel she will do whatever she can do to find a way of peace.

Or perhaps some one of the princes of the kingdom or one of the barons or knights or powerful subjects commits some crime, even against the majesty of his lord, or is to blame for it, and she sees that if he is captured and punished or warred against great evil can come to the land. Similar cases have often been seen in France and other places in episodes involving quite an insignificant baron or knight compared to the king of France (who is a great prince), whence have come many great evils and much harm to the kingdom, as the Chronicles of France relate of the Count of Corbeil*, the lord of Montlhéry† and several others. And it even happened not long ago that my lord Robert d'Artois, by his dispute with the king, greatly harmed the kingdom of France to the benefit of the English.

Since the good lady will bear these things in mind and feel pity

* At the confluence of the Seine and Essonne, this town gave its name to a line of counts who were immediate vassals of the king of France, with whom they often had stormy relations.

† Near Corbeil. When the barons revolted on the accession of Louis IX, Queen Blanche of Castille took refuge with her son in the Château de Montlhéry.

for the destruction of the people, she will wish to work to make peace. She will urge the people, her husband and his council to consider this matter carefully before undertaking it, in view of the evil which could result from it. Any prince ought to avoid as far as he can the spilling of blood, especially that of his own subjects. It is no small matter to undertake a new war, and it ought not to be done without deep reflection and serious deliberation. It would be much better to think of some more suitable way to reach agreement. This lady will not hesitate for a moment, but will speak or have someone else speak (preserving her honour and that of her husband) to the one or ones who have committed the misdeed. She will reproach them for it sharply, saying that the misdeed was very serious and that the prince is quite justifiably offended by it and that he has decided to avenge himself for it, as is only right, but nevertheless she, who would always wish the blessing of peace, in the event that they would wish to atone for it or to make suitable amends, would gladly go to some trouble to try if she could by some means to make peace between them and her husband.

With such words or similar ones, the good princess will always be the means of peace as far as she can be, just as the good Queen Blanche, mother of St Louis, formerly was, who in this manner always exerted herself to make peace between the king and the barons, just as she did with the Count of Champagne and with others. This work is the proper duty of the wise queen and princess: to be the means of peace and concord, to work for the avoidance of war because of the trouble that can come of it. Ladies in particular ought to attend to this business, for men are by nature more courageous and more hot-headed, and the great desire they have to avenge themselves prevents their considering either the perils or the evils that can result from war. But women are by nature more timid and also of a sweeter disposition, and for this reason, if they are wise and if they wish to, they can be the best means of pacifying men. In connection with this, Solomon says in Proverbs in the twenty-fifth chapter: 'By long forbearing is a prince persuaded, and a soft tongue breaketh the bone.' That is, gentle speech softens and breaks its hardness just as the water by its moisture and coldness extinguishes the heat of the fire.

O God, how many great blessings in the world have often been caused by queens and princesses making peace between enemies, between princes and barons and between the rebellious people and their lords! The Scriptures are full of such examples. There is no greater good on earth than the good and wise princess and high-born lady. Happy is the land which has such a one and has had many such. But enough has already been said on this subject in *The Book of the City of Ladies*. And what happens to such princesses? All the subjects feel her to be of such knowledge and goodness that they pledge themselves to her, not only because she is their mistress, but because she seems to them a goddess on earth in whom they have the highest hope and faith, and she is the cause of the country remaining at peace. Her works are not without charity, but rather they are so meritorious that a greater good cannot be done.

9. Of the habits of pious charity that the good princess will cultivate.

By this path, which is Charity, the good princess will travel. But with this in mind she will do still more, as if she took to heart the speech of St Basil when he addressed the rich man: 'If you recognize and confess that temporal wealth has come to you from God, and you know very well, however, that you have received more plentifully than many others who are better than you, you would think for this reason that God, who has not divided the wealth equally, was unjust. However, this ought not to be thought at all, because He has done it so that in giving and distributing to the poor, you can deserve your wealth from God and by his long suffering the poor man can be crowned with the diadem of patience. So ensure that the bread of the hungry does not grow mouldy in your bread bin, that you do not let the side of the naked man be bitten by serpents, that you do not keep the shoes of the barefoot person locked up in your house, and that you do not have in your possession the money of the needy. For know truly that the goods of which you have such an over-abundance belong to the poor and not to you. You are a thief and you steal from God if you are able to go to the aid of your neighbour and yet you do not help him.'

Therefore, the good princess, ever mindful of this principle so that she may accomplish works of mercy, although she may be well established in her grandeur, preserves the virtue of her station. She will have very good ministers around her, for although it is said of princesses that they have bad counsel or bad ministers, I believe that those who are well intentioned have counsellors who would not dare to advise them badly. The master usually seeks out servants according to the sort of person he is; they counsel him well or badly according to what they feel is his will. Therefore, this excellent lady will have servants who accord with her character. She will know that her almoner is a pious, charitable, honourable man without covetousness before she places him in such a position, not at all like some lords, who put the most thievish in positions of authority. God knows what the regime is like of some almoners of lords or prelates entrusted with this duty by that person or by someone else! She will command them to make inquiries in the town and everywhere near by and find out where the houses of the poor are: poor gentlemen or poor gentlewomen sick or fallen on hard times, poor widows, needy householders, poor maidens waiting to marry, women in childbed, students, and poverty-stricken priests or members of religious orders. By the example of my lord St Nicholas she will secretly send gifts to these good people by her almoner, without even the poor themselves knowing who is sending them the alms. The good princess will never be ashamed to visit hospitals and the poor in all her grandeur, accompanied magnificently, as is fitting. She will speak to the poor and to the sick; she will visit their bedsides and will comfort them sweetly, making her excellent and welcome gift of alms. For poor people are much more comforted and accept with more pleasure the kind word, the visit, and the comfort of a great and powerful person than of someone else. The reason for this is that they think that all this world scorns them, and when a powerful person deigns to visit them or to comfort them they feel that they have recovered some honour, which is naturally a thing that everyone desires.

And so when the princess or great lady practises charity, she acquires greater merit than a lesser woman would in the same situation, for three principal reasons. The first is that the greater the person is and the more she humbles herself, the more her goodness increases. The second is that she gives greater aid and comfort to the poor, as has already been said. And the third, which is by no means an unimportant reason, is that she gives a good example to those who see her perform such work and with such great humility, for nothing influences the common people so much as what they see their lord and lady do. Therefore, it is a great benefit when lords and ladies and all other persons who hold positions of authority over others are well brought up, and great mischief when they are not.

Do not by any means imagine that there is a lady so great that it is shameful or in conflict with her rank for her to go herself, devoutly and humbly, on pilgrimages or to visit churches and holy places, nor that such thoughts are misguided, for if she is ashamed of doing good, she is ashamed of saving her soul.

'But,' you will say to me, 'how does the great lady give her alms, and those other things, if she has no money? For you said before that it is dangerous to lay up treasure.' I answer that there is nothing wrong with the princess or great lady amassing treasure of money from revenue or a pension that she receives lawfully and without committing extortion, but what will she do with this treasure? She is certainly not obliged, even according to the Word of God, to give everything to the poor if she does not wish to. She can legitimately keep it for the necessities of her rank and to pay her servants, give gifts when it is appropriate and pay for what is requisitioned on her behalf. Her debts must be paid, for otherwise it would be pointless to distribute alms to others. If the good lady refrains from unnecessary things (which she can easily do if she wishes to) – from having so many gowns and jewels that she does not need – therein lies the pure and right kind of almsgiving and great merit.

Oh, how great and well advised is the lady who does this! She can be compared to the wise man who was once elected to be governor of a city. He was circumspect and noticed that several other men who had been elected to this same office had afterwards been deposed and banished, poor and deprived of all their possessions, in exile in a certain poor country where they died of starvation. He said to himself that he would provide for just such an emergency, so that in case he was sent into exile he would not die of hunger. He managed in such a way the money and wealth that came to him from his earnings and from his revenue while he was in office that after his obligations had been scrupulously met, he put all the remainder aside in a safe place. In the end what happened to the others happened to him, but the provision that he had wisely put aside saved him and kept him from need. Likewise the wealth that is tied up in needless fripperies ought to be used for giving to the poor and doing good. It is the treasure that is set aside in your holy coffer that supplies you after death and keeps you from the exile of Hell. The Gospels emphasize this fact, saying again and again, 'Lay up treasures in Heaven, for alas, the only thing you take with you is this treasure.' It is true, as the Holy Scriptures affirm, that the princess and all women who conscientiously lay up this kind of treasure are undoubtedly excellent managers.

54

To put it briefly, besides the other virtues mentioned above, this noble virtue of charity which, as I have said, will envelop the heart of the good princess, will render her of such very good will towards all people that she will imagine that everyone else is more worthy than she. Since her heart will rejoice as much at the well-being of another as at her own, she will be delighted to hear good reports about other people. To the best of her ability in all things she will give opportunities to the good to persevere and to the bad to reform.

10. Of the moral doctrine that Worldly Prudence will teach the wise princess.

We have sufficiently described the teachings and admonitions that the love and fear of God give the good princess or high-born lady. From now on we must speak of the lessons Worldly Prudence gives her. These teachings and admonitions are not separate from those of God but come from them and are based on them. We will describe wise self-discipline and the prudent way of living.

First of all Prudence teaches the princess or great lady how above all things in this base world she ought to love honour and a good reputation. She will say to her: 'It does not displease God for a person to live in this world morally, and if she lives morally she will love the blessing of a good reputation, which is honour. St Augustine bears witness to this in the *Book of Correction*, which says that two things are necessary to live well: conscience and a good reputation. The wise man in the Book of Ecclesiasticus agrees with this: he says, "Have regard to thy name; for that shall continue with thee above a thousand great treasures of gold."'

For this reason the wise princess will say to herself, 'Above all earthly things, there is nothing that is so becoming to noble people as honour. But what things,' she will ask, 'are necessary for genuine honour?'

'Certainly, properly speaking, it is not worldly riches, at least if they are used according to the common custom of the world; indeed, to be more precise, they are quite the least important thing that goes to perfect one's honour.'

'And what things therefore are more suitable?'

'In truth they are good manners and behaviour.'

'And what is the use of these good manners and behaviour?'

'They perfect the noble person and cause her to be well regarded.

And that is the absolutely perfect honour, for there is no doubt at all that whatever qualities may be in a prince or in a princess or any other person, if he does not lead a life by which he acquires praise, honour and a good reputation by doing good, he entirely lacks honour, although he may be led to think he has it by the flattery of his cronies, for true honour must be without reproach.'

'And how should the great lady love this honour?'

'Certainly more than her life, for she ought to lose it sooner than her honour. There is a good reason for this, for whoever dies well is saved, but whoever is dishonoured is reproached dead and alive forever for as long as there is any memory of her. Oh, what a very great treasure a princess or any other lady has who possesses an honourable reputation! Certainly there is nothing so great in this world that she could have and nothing she should so much love to accumulate, for ordinary treasure is only useful when it is around her person, but that of a good name serves her both near and far, and raises her honour throughout the land. A lady's good reputation is like a great odour from the body of some creature that spreads abroad throughout the world in such a way that all people may smell it. In just this way by the odour of the good reputation, which everywhere flows out from a good person, all people can have the scent of a good example.'

Prudence will advise the wise princess about these things and what she must do to put them into practice. She will arrange her life principally in two areas. The first will be concerned with the manners and behaviour that she wishes to practise, and the second with the manner and order of living that she will wish to establish.

As for the behaviour ensuing from the above-mentioned virtues, two others are especially necessary to the princess and to any great lady, or for that matter to any woman who wishes to have great honour, and without them they cannot obtain it. The one is sobriety and the other is chastity. This sobriety, which is the first, does not extend only to drinking and eating, but to all other areas in which it can help to restrain excesses. This sobriety will make her easy to serve, for she will not want any service more than reason requires, in spite of her high position. It will make her content with such wines and such foods as are put before her, for in this matter she will not insist on having her own way, however modest it may be, and still will take nothing except as much as the necessity of life may strictly require. Sobriety will keep her from sleeping too much, because Prudence will tell her that too great repose engenders sin and vice.

Sobriety will keep her from the vice of avarice, for modest wealth will easily meet her needs without unnecessary and extravagant clothing and all sorts of jewellery. Above all else she will be forbidden to have more magnificence than is reasonable by the admonitions of Prudence, who will doubtless speak to her like this: 'It is most seemly that any princess or land-owning lady, according to her station in life, be richly adorned, as much by garments, dress, ornaments, and jewels, as by a great court with courtiers and much ceremony due to the honour of the position where God has placed her. But do not doubt for a moment that if you (or anyone else) are not content with such rank and clothing as your noble forebears have enjoyed and you want to have something greater or to make innovations, you are making a mistake and act against your honour and against the good of sobriety. Therefore, do not do it, for it is not seemly for anyone to do this kind of thing; indeed, even if a lady's husband, whom she ought to obey and comply with and by whom she ought to be ruled, wishes it, she still ought not to undertake anything without serious thought, counsel, and a good reason.'

This sobriety shows in the lady's good sense as well as in the external deeds and clothing, for it will make her countenance grave without being vacant, and it will keep her from too much enthusiasm and from many sweet scents (to which many ladies have devoted great attention and have spent an abundance of money on them). Prudence will tell her one ought not to give the body so many little luxuries, and it is better that such money be given to the poor and indigent. In addition this Sobriety will so correct, chastise and control the mouth and the speech of the wise lady, whom she will keep principally from talking too much (which is a most unseemly thing in a noble lady, or in any woman of quality), that she will hate with all her heart the vice of lying. She will love truth, which will be so habitually in her mouth that people will believe what she says and have confidence in her as one has in a lady whom one has never heard lie. This virtue of truth is more becoming in the mouth of a prince and of a princess than in that of other people because it is right that everyone should believe them. Sobriety will prevent her from saying any word, especially in a place where it could be passed on and reported, that she has not well examined. Prudence and Sobriety will teach the lady to have controlled speech and sensible eloquence, neither too solemn nor too frivolous, but sweet, calm and composed. She will speak rather softly and with a pleasant expression without making grimaces or movements of the body or the hands. Sobriety will keep her from laughing too much and without cause. It will prevent her, above all else, from ever speaking badly of any other person or saying any word of criticism, but rather she will always emphasize the good, and willingly keep a tight rein on empty and indecent words and never say them.

In all her gaiety and pastimes it will become her to preserve all moderation and modesty. She should say to her serving-women and serving-girls, or to others according to the occasion, virtuous and exemplary words, so that those men and women who hear them will say that this speech issues from a very good, wise and chaste lady. Sobriety will keep her from speaking to her women and servants ungraciously, or scolding or saying base things. She will teach them kindly and correct their faults, courteously warning them that she may dismiss them or punish them in some way if they do not improve. However, her speech will always be calm and without coarseness, because when coarseness issues from the mouth of a lady or of any woman it rebounds more on her herself than on those to whom she says it. She will make her commands reasonable in place and in time, and to those whose business it is, each in his own duties. This lady will gladly read instructive books about good manners and behaviour and sometimes devotion, but those about indecency and lubricity she will utterly hate and not wish to have at her court. She will not permit them to be brought into the presence of any girl, female relative or woman in her court, for there is no doubt at all that the examples of good or evil influence the minds of those men or women who see or hear them. And so this noble lady takes pleasure in recording and saying good words and especially the Word of God, for the godly woman will hear His Word eagerly in the manner that He describes in the Gospel, where He says, 'Those who love me hear my word willingly and keep it.' She will often hear sermons by notable and good preachers and inspirational readings at feasts and at other times. Similarly, she will want her girls and women and all her family to be there. She will want to be well informed of everything that touches our articles of faith and commandments and everything that pertains to salvation. Of worldly affairs, she will gladly hear about worthwhile people, worthy knights and gentlemen, their deeds and their exploits, great clergymen and their knowledge, all upright men and all worthy women, their intelligence and their good lives. She will love them and welcome them warmly; she will do them great honour and give them handsome gifts.

Furthermore, she will get to know people of good and upright lives who are devoted to God, and she will want them to be her friends. She will receive them humbly and speak to them confidentially and very willingly hear them and ask them to pray for her. In this way the virtue of sobriety will rule the good princess.

This rule is followed by the second of the two virtues that we have said she will particularly wish to have, that is, chastity, which she will have so abundantly and with such purity that in neither word nor deed, appearance, ornaments, nor bearing, conduct, social pomp nor expression will there be anything for which she could be reproached or criticized.

11. The way of life of the wise princess, shown by the admonition of Prudence.

Prudence, as I have said before, will advise the wise princess how her life should be ordered, and as a result she will adopt the following way of life. She will rise quite early every day and address her first words to God, saying, 'Lord, I beseech thee to guard us this day from sin, from sudden death and from all evil mischance, and also protect all our relatives and friends. To those who have passed on, pardon, and to our subjects peace and tranquillity. Amen, Pater Noster.' She will say such additional prayers as her devotion may prompt her to, but she will not insist on having a great attendance of servants around her. (The good and wise Queen Jeanne, the late wife of King Charles V of France, followed this course when she was alive. She rose every morning before daylight, lit her candle herself to say her prayers, and did not allow any woman of hers to get up or to lose sleep on her account.)

When the lady is ready she will go to hear her Masses, as many as accord with her devotion and as time and leisure will permit her. For there is no doubt that this lady, to whom great powers to govern are entrusted, will merit the trust that many lords have, and have had, in their wives when they see that they are good and prudent and they themselves have to go away to be occupied elsewhere. The husbands give them the responsibility and authority to govern and to be head of the council. Such ladies are more to be excused in the eyes of God if they do not spend so much time in long prayers as those who have more leisure, nor do they have less merit in attending conscientiously to public affairs than those who occupy themselves more with prayers (unless they intend to devote themselves to the contemplative life and leave the active life). But as I have said before, the contemplative life can manage quite well without the active, but the good and proper active life cannot function without some part of the contemplative. This lady will have such a good, orderly system that as she leaves her chapel there will be some poor people at the door to whom she herself with humility and devotion will give alms from her own hand, and if any deserving petitions are made to her, she will hear them kindly and give a gracious reply. She will not detain those that she can deal with quickly, and she will therefore increase her alms and also her great renown. If she perhaps cannot consider all the requests that are made to her, certain gentlemen will be appointed to hear them. She will wish them to be charitable and work quickly, and she herself will watch over their conduct.

When she has done these things, if she has responsibility of government, she will go to the council on days when it is held. There she will have such a bearing, such a manner and such an expression when she is seated in her high seat that she will indeed seem to be the lady and mistress over all, and everyone will hold her in great reverence as their wise mistress with great authority. She will conscientiously hear the proposals that are put forward and listen to everyone's opinion. She will be so attentive that she will grasp the principal points and conclusions of matters and will note carefully which of her counsellors speak better and with the best deliberation and advice, and which seem to her the most prudent and intelligent. And she will also note, in the diversity of opinions, which causes and which reasons most stir the speakers. In this way she will attend to everything, and when someone comes to her to speak on a subject or to reply, according to the circumstances, so wisely will she consider the matter that she cannot be thought simple or ignorant. If she can find out in advance what someone is going to propose and what the ramifications of it may be, and if she can with wise counsel think of a suitable reply, it is all to the good. Furthermore, this lady will establish a certain number of wise gentlemen who will sit on her council, who she will deem good, loyal, virtuous and not too covetous. A great many princes and princesses are put to shame by counsellors filled with covetousness, for according to their own inclinations they incite and encourage those whom they counsel. Inevitably, those who indulge in such vice counsel neither well nor loyally, neither to the profit of their souls nor to the honour of their bodies, and so the prudent lady must inquire whether they lead virtuous lives. She will be counselled every day by these gentlemen at a certain hour about the necessary matters that she has to deal with.

After the morning council she will have her midday meal, which ordinarily and especially on solemn days and on feast days will be in the hall, where the ladies and maidens are seated, and other suitable persons ranked according to their position at court. There she will be served in a manner befitting her rank, and while the plates are still on the table (according to the fine old custom of queens and princesses) she will have a gentleman at hand who will speak of the deeds of some good deceased person, or he will speak on some excellent moral subject or tell stories of exemplary lives. No dispute will be conducted there. After the tables have been taken up and grace has been said, if there are any princes or lords present, if there are any ladies or damsels or other visitors around her, then she will receive each of them in such honour as is fitting so that everyone will feel contented. She will speak to them in a thoughtful manner, with a pleasant expression; to the elderly people in a more serious manner, to the young people in a different and merrier one. And if one happens to say or to hear any amusing thing or any merriment she will know how to contain it with such a pleasant manner that everyone will say that she is a gracious lady and one who well knows her manners in all places.

After the spices have been taken and it is time to retire, the lady will go to her chamber, where she will rest for a short while if she feels the need to. Then afterwards, if it is a weekday and she has no other more important occupation with which to avoid idleness, she will take up some work, and she will have the women and girls around her work similarly. In the privacy of her chamber she will wish each of them to choose freely whatever she likes from all respectable kinds of merriment, and she herself will laugh with them and divert herself in private gatherings so unconstrainedly that they will all praise her great liberty and indulgence and they will love her with all their hearts. She will be occupied like this until the hour of vespers, when she will go to hear them in her chapel if it is a feast day and if no weighty business prevents her, or otherwise she will say them without fail with her lady chaplain. After doing this, if it is summer, she will go off to amuse herself in a garden until supper-time, walking up and down for her health. She will wish that if any persons need to see her for any reason they be allowed to enter and she will hear them. At bedtime she will pray to God. And that concludes the schedule of the ordinary day of the prudent princess living in good and holy occupation.

As for other amusements in which ladies are accustomed to take their pleasure (like going hunting, sometimes hunting with a falcon by the river for aquatic game, or other pastimes), we do not add these things to the order of our discipline and teaching, for we leave them to the preference and desire of their husbands and themselves. A certain amount of latitude can well be given to these things in time and in place, even by very virtuous ladies, without blame, but it should not be excessive, and moderation should always be maintained.

12. *Of the seven principal teachings of Prudence that any princess who loves honour must remember. The first is how to conduct herself towards her husband, in general and in particular.*

Now we have said enough in general terms, first of all about devotion towards God, and then the good manners ladies ought to have, and the ordering of their way of life. Now we would like to advance for their edification seven principal teachings, which according to Prudence are necessary to those who desire to live wisely and wish to have honour. We beg them (and similarly all ladies – great, middling or little – to whom this may pertain) to note and put into effect these seven teachings, for knowledge is worth nothing to those who do not put it into practice.

The first of these seven rules that is seemly for every lady (and likewise every married woman) is that she love her husband and live in peace with him, or otherwise she will have already discovered the torments of Hell, where there is nothing but violence and tumult. As it is quite clear that many women of all classes, although they love their husbands dearly, do not know all the rules of conduct (either through youth or for some other reason), here is our lesson, which will explain the matter thoroughly.

The noble princess who would like to follow the rule of honour in all circumstances will behave towards her lord, be he old or young, in all the ways that good faith and true love command. That is, she will humble herself towards him, in deed and word and by curtsying; she will obey without complaint; and she will hold her peace to the best of her ability in the way that the good and wise Queen Esther did, as it is written in the Bible in the first chapter of the Book of Esther. She was for this reason so loved and honoured by her lord that he denied her nothing that she desired. In addition the princess will demonstrate love by being careful and fastidious in all the things that might pertain to the well-being of her husband, both of his soul and his body. Of the soul: because she is on friendly terms with her confessor, if she sees in her husband any spot of foul sin, of which the habit could lead him to damnation, and she does not dare to mention it for fear that he might be displeased with her and also that it is none of her business, she will have her confessor tell him. She will ask him to be sure to remind him to be always a servant of Our Lord in all things, including all his alms and good deeds. She will say, 'Pray to God for my husband and for me.'

Besides the provision for the soul, this lady will be very solicitous about her husband's body so that he may be maintained in health and preserved in long life. She will often want to speak to his physicians and inquire of them about his state of health. Sensible wife that she is, she will often want to hear their opinions and sometimes compare them on the subject of her husband's health.

She will want to know how he is served, and to this end she will feel no shame in keeping a careful eye on those whose duty it is to serve him. Since it is not the custom among the higher nobility for ladies to be as commonly in the presence of their husbands as other women are their own husbands, she will often inquire of the chamberlains and of others who are around him about his well-being. She will be overjoyed to see him, and when she is with him she will try hard to say everything that ought to please him, and she will keep a happy expression on her face.

But some may perhaps answer us here that we are not taking into account certain defects and that we are talking utter nonsense. They may argue that we are saying that come what may ladies ought to love their husbands very much and show the signs of it, but that we are not saying anything about whether they all deserve to be treated so well by their wives. It is well known that there are some husbands who behave very distantly towards their wives and give no sign of love, or very little. We reply to them that our teaching in this present work is not addressed to men, although some of them need it if they would be well instructed. Because we speak so exclusively to women, we set out for their profit both to teach the valuable methods of avoiding dishonour and to give good advice for following the right course of action.

Suppose that the husband, of whatever class he may be, has extremely perverse and rude behaviour. Suppose he is unloving towards his wife or strays into a love affair with some other woman. If the wife cannot remedy the situation, she must put up with all this and dissimulate wisely, pretending that she does not notice it and that she truly does not know anything about it. As a prudent woman, she will think, 'If you speak to him harshly you will gain nothing, and if he leads you a bad life you will be kicking against the spur; he will perhaps leave you, and people will mock you all the more and believe shame and dishonour, and it may be still worse for you. You must live and die with him whatever he is like.'

Having considered these things, the wise lady will go to some trouble to keep his interest by being pleasant and kind, and if she knows that it is best to mention something to him, she will bring it up sweetly and tactfully when they are alone together. Sometimes she will admonish him out of devotion, at other times out of the kindness that she owes him, and at still other times while smiling, as though she were making a joke of it. Besides this, she will have good people and her confessor speak to him. In addition to these things, the noble lady will excuse him if she hears other people talking about him. She will not be able to endure hearing anything bad said of him, and so she will not care for gossips to report anything about him. Virtuously, as a prudent and wise lady ought to do, she will forbid it, for she will consider the matter and then will conclude that she would have only sadness from any such knowledge and would gain nothing from it.

When she has followed this course of action for a time and has seen that he does not want to change his ways, she will take refuge in God. She will do everything she can to be resigned to the situation without saying anything more to him about it. And this lady or woman, whoever she may be, may be certain that such a perverse man will feel remorse only late in life. Then Reason will say to him, 'You have committed a great sin against your good and virtuous wife,' and that he should reform and love her as much as or more than those who never stray from the right path. Eventually she will have won her cause through steadfastly enduring.

And if it happens that her husband should go on any distant or perilous voyage, or to some war, the good lady will pray devoutly to God and scrupulously have people pray for him in processions and oblations. She will increase the number of her alms. She will dress humbly and simply and keep outward show to a minimum during this time, and on his return she will receive him with great joy and honour. To all his company she will give a joyous welcome, and she will eagerly want to hear about the best of his men, the most noble and the most valiant. She will want to know how they are, and very gladly she will hear their adventures recounted. She will receive them with great honour and give them fine gifts. She will also want to know how those who had the care of his body did their duty and how they treated him.

She will praise the best and most conscientious men. It is greatly to the honour of a lady to behave in this way and to say these things sincerely. She will want her behaviour to be apparent and known to everyone and not at all kept secret, because she loves honour and a good reputation. Prudence will teach her that no greater honour can be said of a lady or any woman than that she is true and loyal to her husband, and that she clearly shows that she loves him and consequently is loyal to him (for it is commonly thought that a woman who truly loves her husband will not be false to him). She cannot give any proof of her loyalty except by the love that she shows him and the external signs by which thoughts and emotions are commonly judged. One cannot judge the intention of good people except by their deeds, which if they are good testify to a good person, and vice versa.

This will suffice for this first lesson, which is suitable for any good woman, whoever she may be.

13. The second teaching of Prudence, which is how the wise princess conducts herself towards the relatives and friends of her husband.

The second teaching that Prudence demonstrates to the princess (and generally to every sensible woman) is that if she values her honour, she will want everyone to know that she loves her husband. She will love and honour the relatives of her husband and show it in the following ways. She will honour them and make them all very welcome when they come to visit, and when other people are present she will honour her husband's family more than her own. She will try in all reasonable and lawful ways to please them and be obliging to them. She will win them over amiably and with a happy disposition. She will intervene on their behalf with her husband if the need arises, and if there should be any dispute between them she will do her utmost to make peace. She will speak well of them and praise them. She will not allow herself to be drawn into arguments, and in every way she will avoid as far as possible any contention or rancour arising between her and them. If one of her in-laws is stand-offish and uncivil, she will try her best to break down this reserve according to her position and the preservation of her honour.

She will love not only the relatives of her husband, but also all those whom she knows that he loves. But suppose now that she finds out that some of them have bad characters; she will still be friendly towards them because she cannot make them good, nor can she probably prevent or deflect the love or hate that her husband feels for anyone. There would be nothing but dispute and quarrelling if she showed them ill will, and she would acquire that many more enemies. People would say that it was quite true that a wife would never love anyone whom her husband loved. However, if she knows that her husband tends to believe her, and if she is certain that his friends are vicious and bad and that her husband may become wicked in deed or in habit through associating with them, she will speak to him about it discreetly and gently when they are alone together, or she will have someone else tell him.

If she develops these habits, her husband will hold her in great favour. She will have the favour and benevolence of his relatives, who will hold her in high esteem and protect her from many dangers and difficulties. She will be more secure when she has the favour of the relatives of her husband, for one has very often seen women greatly harmed by their husbands' relatives. This evidence (along with others) will give a still greater proof of the love and loyalty that she has for her husband.

14. The third teaching of Prudence, which is how the wise princess will carefully watch over the welfare and upbringing of her children.

The third teaching of Prudence to the wise princess is that if she has children she should watch over them and their upbringing diligently, even the sons, although it is the father's responsibility to seek a teacher for them and take on such governors as are good and suitable. Although the lady perhaps does not care for so much responsibility, as it is the nature of a mother commonly to be more involved with the care of her children, she ought to consider carefully everything that pertains to them, but more to that which touches discipline and teaching than to the training of the body.

The wise princess will take care how they are disciplined, and she will be very interested in those who have charge of them, and how they carry out their duties. She will not wait for a report from someone else, but she herself will often visit her children in their rooms. She will see them go to bed and get up and see how they are disciplined. It is no dishonour for a princess to do such things, for children are the greatest haven, security and ornament that she can have. It often happens that someone would greatly like to harm the mother but would not dare to do it out of fear of the children; she ought to hold them very dear. It is great praise to say that she is careful about them, for it is a sign that she is wise and good.

Therefore, the wise lady who loves her children dearly will be diligent about their education. She will ensure that they will learn first of all to serve God, and to read and write, and that the teacher will be careful to make them learn their prayers well. The wise lady will try to get the children's father to agree that they be introduced to Latin and that they understand something of the sciences. This instruction is very suitable for the children of princes and lords. When they grow older and have some understanding, she will also want them to be apprised of practical matters, government and everything princes should know about. She will want them to be told and shown all the precepts of virtue and taught the way to avoid vices. This lady will pay close attention to the behaviour and wisdom of the teacher and others who come in contact with her children. She will have them removed if they are not good and replace them with others.

She will want her children to be brought to her often. She will consider their appearance, actions and speech and she will correct them severely herself if they misbehave. She will make them respect her and she will want them to do her great honour. She will converse with them in order to sense their understanding and their knowledge, and she will teach them wisely. Her daughters will be governed by good and wise ladies, and before she commits their upbringing to anyone, she will look into her attitudes, behaviour and life, for she must be very watchful about this matter. She must see that the lady or maiden to whom she entrusts the care of her daughter is of good reputation, devout and intelligent. She should be from a good family, and she should be wise and prudent so that she knows how to demonstrate the good manners and deportment fitting for the daughter of a prince. This governess ought to be mature, so that she may be all the more wise in her habits and more esteemed and respected, even by the child whom she governs, and also by all those members of the court with more authority and power. A lady who has such a responsibility should take great care that there is no girl or woman around the prince's daughter of whom any reproach is known nor one who is of low rank, frivolous, silly or bad mannered, so that the child cannot follow any bad example. When the girl is old enough, the princess will wish her to learn to read. After she knows her religious offices and the Mass, she can be given books of devotion and contemplation or ones dealing with good behaviour. The princess will not tolerate books containing any vain things, follies or dissipation to be brought before her daughter, for the doctrine and teaching that the girl absorbs in her early childhood she usually remembers all her life. As the wise princess watches over the upbringing and education of her daughters, the older they get the more careful she will be. She will have them around her most of the time and keep them respectful. Her prudent behaviour and virtue will be an example to her daughters to govern themselves similarly.

15. *The fourth teaching of Prudence, which is how the princess will maintain a discreet manner towards those who do not like her and are envious of her.*

The fourth lesson of Prudence to the wise princess is of quite a different order from the previous ones. Much as it differs from the last point, it is no less important to the general knowledge of how to conduct oneself. For the last point is natural, as it is customary for all wise mothers to assume responsibility for the upbringing and education of their children, but to know how to master and correct one's own heart and will is a thing beyond nature. As it is harder to do, it is correspondingly worthier of commendation, and the person who well knows how to put it into practice is more to be praised, for it is a sign of very great strength and steadfastness of heart, which is one of the most excellent cardinal virtues. It is an absolute necessity for all wise ladies and princesses who love the prize of honour, praise and a good name to know how to use this strength, or otherwise their prudence can neither make itself known nor be seen to the best advantage nor be perfect.

Let me put it another way: there is not the least doubt that, according to the way of the world and the movements of fortune, there is no prince so grand in this world, however just he may be, nor was there ever a lord or lady or any other man or woman who was loved by everybody. Let us imagine a person who is altogether perfect – he would not suffer the despicable resentment that fixes itself in the human heart when he was pleasant to everyone but still not loved by everybody. We can see this principle in the person of Jesus Christ, who alone was perfect, and yet Envy killed Him, as it has many good and valiant people that I could mention. The better and more virtuous a lady is, the greater the war Envy very often makes against her. There is no man or woman so powerful (nor ever was, except God) who could avenge himself for every affront. Therefore, the wise princess, and similarly all those who wish to act prudently, will be aware of this problem and provide themselves with a remedy. If Fortune should wish to assail her in any place (as it has done and does to many good people) and she finds out that some powerful person or persons do not wish her well, dislike her, and would harm her if they could and alienate her from the love and favour of her husband (who would believe them perhaps for their blandishments and flatteries), or by their false reports would portray her badly to barons, subjects or people, she will not make any sign that she notices it nor that she considers them her enemies. Rather, by being friendly to them she will make them think that she regards them highly as her friends and would never believe that they might be otherwise. They will think that she has more trust in them than in anyone else. But she should be so wise and circumspect that no one can perceive that she does it calculatingly. It would be shameful if at one time she was very cordial and another time gave them furious looks that seemed genuine and were so plain that it was clear that her smile was insincere. The sensible thing is to observe moderation in this matter, and it is indeed necessary to be prepared for the situation before it arises. She will pretend that she wishes to defer to them and their advice, and she will summon them to confidential meetings (as she will pretend them to be), where she will tell them ordinary things with a great show of secrecy and confidence and keep her real thoughts to herself. It is best to do this with the appearance of sincerity so that it does not put them on their guard.

She should not talk carelessly, for if she said anything about them behind their backs contrary to the impression she wished to give and word of it got back to them, it would be a dangerous situation. No lord or lady is so great that all their servants are loyal, and so they ought to be careful who might overhear them. With a heart that is large and full, a lady cannot always keep quiet about what displeases her, but if she let slip a wrong word she might ruin her whole project. It would reflect shame on her and diminish her standing if her enemies got to know that she had found out that they did not like her, but she still pretended to them that she did not know. They would think that she had done it out of fear, and it would make them prouder and bolder to harm her, and they would think less of her because of it. A lady must know how to prevent this from happening.

If any person should report anything to her about others and she thinks that her response may be reported back to them, she will rebuke this person and say that she knows very well that they would wish her well-being and her honour, and that they are very good and loyal friends. Let us suppose that these enemies should do or say something to her prejudice. She can gloss over it by saying that they must have done or said it for some other reason than malice towards her. Again, she will pretend to be so simple or ignorant that she does not notice it and pretend that it has nothing to do with her and that she has no inkling or suspicion against them. But in spite of all these things and her great dissimulations, she will watch them as carefully as she can and stay on her guard.

Thus the wise lady will use this discreet pretence and prudent caution, which is not to be thought a vice, but is a great virtue when it is done in the cause of goodness and peace without injuring anyone in order to avoid a greater misfortune. She will avoid evil and reap benefits if she gives the appearance of not being aware of their offences. If she acknowledged them, it would cause her to have arguments and quarrels with her enemies and try to avenge herself. She would be obliged to seek satisfaction, making her friends unhappy and placing them in a dangerous position. Her husband or the other barons and subjects might believe them more than her, and that would then make the quarrel worse and give rise to greater mischief. If she did not yet feel properly avenged, she would have all the greater sorrow. By using the method I have described of patience and dissimulation, she can be confident of placating the anger and spite of all her enemies, and at the very least they will never dare to harm her as much as if she had shown herself to be their enemy. It is common sense that anyone would be very disloyal and ill bred to want to do wrong in any way to the person who regarded him as a friend.

But let us suppose that they continue their treachery: their wickedness will be very much greater, and more apparent to everyone. They will be all the more condemned for it and also much more dishonoured, as you are supposed to be their friend. They will fall short of their object, for everyone will consider them in the wrong, and in such a situation the lady inevitably gains more in the long run by maintaining so long-suffering a manner than by being vengeful. There is no doubt that this teaching is suitable for princesses and ladies but also generally for all women, for many quarrels do indeed come in marriage because of false reports of deceivers to husbands, because many women cannot pretend to ignore certain things, or do not know how to do it well. God knows this, among others!

16. *The fifth teaching of Prudence, which is how the wise princess will try her best to be in favour with, and have the good wishes of, all classes of her subjects.*

As it is fitting for the wise and prudent princess to wish to regulate her actions so that she seeks and follows all the paths that honour demands, she will want for this reason (which is the fifth teaching) to enjoy the favour of the clergy and to be on good terms with persons in religious orders, leaders of the Church, prelates and councillors, as well as the middle classes and even the common people. No one can be surprised that we say she should especially cultivate these people more than the barons and nobles. The reason for this is that we suppose that she already associates with barons and nobles, for it would be according to the common custom for her to be acquainted with them. She wishes to be in favour with the above-mentioned persons for two reasons.

The first is so that the good and devout will pray to God for her, and the second is that she may be praised by them in their sermons and homilies so that, if the need arises, their voices and words can be a shield and defence against the rumours and reports of her slanderous enemies and can negate them. By this strategy she will have more of her husband's love and also that of the common people, who will hear good things about their lady, and also she may be supported by the most powerful people in an emergency. She will find out which of the clerks and scholars, those in religious orders as well as others, will be the most useful and of the greatest authority and in whom and in whose word people place the most confidence. Those persons will inspire the others with confidence in her. She will speak to them all very amiably and want to have their advice and make use of it. She will sometimes ask them to dinner at her court, together with her confessor and the people of her chapel, who will all be honourable people. She will accord them great honour and will wish them to be honoured by her household, which is a very seemly thing, for truly those who are ennobled by learning ought to be honoured. She will do them all the good in her power and contribute to their colleges and monasteries.

Although almsgiving should be done secretly (the reason for this is so that the person who gives them may not be puffed up with pride about it, for that is a mortal sin), if she did not feel any pride in her heart, it would be better to give publicly than in secret, because she would set a good example to others. Whoever does it in this frame of mind doubles her merit and does well. This wise lady who knows how to protect herself from this vice will indeed wish that the gifts and alms that she gives in this way will be known and recorded (if they are notable, such as for rebuilding churches and monasteries or some other necessary thing) in perpetual memory on tablets in their churches so that the people will pray to God for her. Or her name may appear on other lists of benefactors, or her gifts may be announced publicly. Others will follow her example and give similarly, and by their actions they will gain a good reputation. It may seem that she has a small streak of hypocrisy or that she is getting a name for it, yet it may be called a 'just hypocrisy', so to speak, for it strives towards good and the avoidance of evil. We do not mean that under cover of almsgiving they ought to commit evil deeds and sin, nor that great vanity ought to arise in their hearts. Certainly being 'hypocritical' in the cause of good will not offend any person who desires honour. We repeat that this kind of 'just hypocrisy' is almost necessary, especially to princes and princesses who must rule over others and to whom more reverence is due than to other people. As for that, it is written in the book of Valerius* that formerly princes claimed that they were descended from the gods so that their subjects would hold them in greater reverence and fear them more.

The wise lady will wish her husband's counsellors to think well of her, be they prelates, chancellors or others. She will command them to come to her. She will receive them honourably and speak to them intelligently. As best she can, she will try to be worthy of their great esteem. This approach will be valuable to her in several ways. They will

* Probably Valerius Antias, the Roman annalist (fl. 70 BC).

praise her good sense and conduct, which they will regard as outstanding. If it happens that any envious person wishes to intrigue against her, they will not allow any decisions to be made to her prejudice. They will dissuade the prince if he has been misinformed by any other people. If she desired anything to be discussed in council they would be more friendly and favourable to her.

In addition, this lady will wish to have the good will of the clergy, who become embroiled with the 'common causes' of the people, as we say in Paris, with advocates in Parliament and elsewhere. She will wish to see such defenders of causes on certain days, the leaders and principal men among them and the other most notable ones. She will confer with them amiably and want them to understand her honourable position. She will do this not so that she may speak to them from motives of vengeance, but so that they should perceive the effect of her conduct and great knowledge. To have such a custom can be valuable for the increase of her honour and praise. The reason for this is that she will wish all sorts and conditions of the legal fraternity, the leading citizens of towns and cities in her husband's jurisdiction, and also great merchants and even some of the most respectable artisans to come to her from time to time. She will welcome them warmly and try hard to be well regarded by them, so that if she were to have any difficulty and if she needed some ready money, these merchants, being well disposed towards her, would gladly help her. If she must borrow and if she wishes to honour her commitments, she ought to render payment without fail on the appointed day. If she always keeps her word sincerely and unswervingly, people will consequently believe in it.

While we have been telling in this chapter how the wise princess ought to be well regarded by her subjects, it could seem wrong to some readers to say such a pointless thing. They might think that it was not the princess's business to court her subjects, but rather she ought to command her pleasures boldly, and her subjects ought to obey and take pains to court *her* love and not the other way around, or otherwise they will not be subjects and she the mistress. But to this we will reply that, with no disrespect to the speakers, it is appropriate to do this, not only for princesses but for princes. There are many reasons, but we will discuss only two, for this matter could be enlarged upon much more. The first reason is that although the prince may be lord and master of his subjects, the subjects nevertheless make the lord and not the lord the subjects. They would very much more easily find someone who would take them on as subjects (if they wished to overthrow him) than he would find people who would receive him as lord! And for this reason, and also because he would not be able to overcome them by himself if they rebelled against him (and even if he then had the power to destroy them, he would forbear to do it), he must necessarily keep their affection, not by harshness but in such a way that from this love comes fear, or otherwise his authority is in peril. The common proverb is quite true that avers, 'There is no lord of a land who is hated by his men.' As for keeping their affection, truly one who sincerely wishes to be called 'lord' could do nothing more sensible, for he could have neither city nor fortress of such a great defensive strength and power as the love and benevolence of true subjects.

The other reason is that, supposing that the subjects feel good will towards the prince and princess, if they never have the courage to go freely to their rulers and if they have never been invited to do so, it would not be their place to begin. Therefore, the prince or princess ought to make the overture. It is perfectly natural for the subjects to celebrate this with great joy and consider themselves quite honoured by it. It ought to double their love and loyalty, and they will then find still more kindness from their rulers. Speaking on this subject, a wise man has said that there is nothing that wins over the hearts of a ruler's subjects more nor that draws them to their lord so much as when they find gentleness and kindness in him, such as is written of a good emperor who said that he wished to behave towards his subjects in such a manner that they themselves would desire him to be their emperor. Bearing this firmly in mind, the wise princess will sometimes invite the wives to visit her, and she will make them very welcome and speak to everyone so amiably that they will be very content and praise her wisdom. Her whole court will celebrate their lyings-in and the weddings of their children, and the princess will wish the women to be in the company of ladies and damsels. From all this she will acquire much love from all men and women.

17. The sixth teaching: how the wise princess will keep the women of her court in good order.

The sixth teaching of Prudence is that, just as the good shepherd takes care that his lambs are maintained in health, and if any of them becomes mangy, separates it from the flock for fear that it may infect the others, so the princess will take upon herself the responsibility for the care of her women servants and companions, who she will ensure are all good and chaste, for she will not want to have any other sort of person around her. Since it is the established custom that knights and squires and all men (especially certain men) who associate with women have a habit of pleading for love tokens from them and trying to seduce them, the wise princess will so enforce her regulations that there will be no visitor to her court so foolhardy as to dare to whisper privately with any of her women or give the appearance of seduction. If he does it or if he is noticed giving any sign of it, immediately she should take such an attitude towards him that he will not dare to importune them any more. The lady who is chaste will want all her women to be so too, on pain of being banished from her company.

She will want them to amuse themselves with decent games, such that men cannot mock, as they do the games of some women, though at the time the men laugh and join in. The women should restrain themselves with seemly conduct among knights and squires and all men. They should speak demurely and sweetly and, whether in dances or other amusements, divert and enjoy themselves decorously and without wantonness. They must not be frolicsome, forward, or boisterous in speech, expression, bearing or laughter. They must not go about with their heads raised like wild deer. This kind of behaviour would be very unseemly and greatly derisory in a woman of the court, in whom there should be more modesty, good manners and courteous behaviour than in any others, for where there is most honour there ought to be the most perfect manners and behaviour. Women of the court in any country would be deceiving themselves very much if they imagined that it was more appropriate for them to be frolicsome and saucy than for other women. For this reason we hope that in time to come our doctrine in this book may be carried into many kingdoms, so that it may be valuable in all places where there might be any shortcoming.

We say generally to all women of all countries that it is the duty of every lady and maiden of the court, whether she be young or old, to be more prudent, more decorous, and better schooled in all things than other women. The ladies of the court ought to be models of all good things and all honour to other women, and if they do otherwise they will do no honour to their mistress nor to themselves. In addition, so that everything may be consistent in modesty, the wise princess will wish that the clothing and the ornaments of her women, though they be appropriately beautiful and rich, be of a modest fashion, well fitting and seemly, neat and properly cared for. There should be no deviation from this modesty nor any immodesty in the matter of plunging necklines or other excesses.

In all things the wise princess will keep her women in order just as the good and prudent abbess does her convent, so that bad reports about it may not circulate in the town, in distant regions or anywhere else. This princess will be so feared and respected because of the wise management that she will be seen to practise that no man or woman will be so foolhardy as to disobey her commands in any respect or to question her will, for there is no doubt that a lady is more feared and respected and held in greater reverence when she is seen to be wise and chaste and of firm behaviour. But there is nothing wrong or inconsistent in her being kind and gentle, for the mere look of the wise lady and her subdued reception is enough of a sign to correct those men and women who err and to inspire them with fear.

18. *The seventh teaching describes how the wise princess will keep a careful eye on her revenues and finances and on the state of her court.*

The seventh teaching of Prudence to the wise princess is that she will carefully look after her revenue and her expenditure, which not only princes and princesses ought to consider, but likewise all people who wish their lives to be regulated by wisdom. She herself will feel no shame in wishing to know the sum of her revenues or payments; on certain days she will have her collectors and the administrators of her finances do their accounts in her presence. She will want to know how the masters of her household govern their staffs, command their underlings and distribute food. In the same way the princess will want to be familiar with other departments of her court. She will want to know that all her officers, whether great or little, are prudent, lead a good life and are the true gentlemen that she takes them for. If she finds out the contrary, she will immediately dismiss them.

She will want to know what the household expenses are. She will want to know what has been bought for her out of her funds from merchants and from her subjects, and she will command that the bills be fully paid on a certain day, for she will certainly not want the curses or the ill will of creditors. She will wish to owe nothing; she will prefer to manage with less and to spend her money more moderately. She will not permit anyone to take anything from the people against their will or at an unfair price, and she will stipulate that her staff must pay promptly and not oblige the poor people of the villages and other places, at great expense and trouble, to come time and time again to deliver a memorandum of a debt to her private apartments or to her finance officers before they are paid. She will not want her treasurers or stewards to be liars, as is the common custom, nor to put the people off with hollow promises and one delay after another.

This wise lady will organize the management of her revenues in the following manner. She will divide her income into five parts. The first will be the portion that she wants to devote to alms and give to the poor. The second part is her household expenses: she will know what the total amounts to – indeed, if need be, she should find out what it is and request her husband not to settle the accounts without involving her in the transaction. The third part is for payment to her officers and women servants. The fourth is for gifts to strangers or others who are particularly deserving of them. And the fifth part she will save and use when she decides to spend something on herself for jewels, gowns and other clothing. Each portion of the amount will be what she sees that she can afford according to her revenue. By means of this rule she will be able to keep her affairs orderly and without confusion, nor will she lack money to fulfil any of the above-mentioned items. For this reason she needs to have some ready money in reserve, and that would not be possible if she had indulged in lavish expenditure and waste.

In this manner the princess will be able to follow the above seven teachings of Prudence, with the other virtues. These things are not at all hard to do, but rather are agreeable and pleasant provided that she is sincere and that she has made something of a habit of them. The wise lady will be able to acquire glory, renown and great honour in this world and eventually in Paradise, which is promised to those who live virtuously.

19. How the wise princess ought to extend largesse and liberality.

As we have spoken at some length about the other virtues appropriate to princesses and we have touched only briefly on a suitable generosity in gifts outside her ordinary expenditure, and as it is out of the ordinary and is something about which a princess ought to be informed, we will now treat it at greater length.

The wise princess wishing to be without reproach will take special care that neither the vice of meanness and avarice may be seen in her, nor foolish generosity, which is no less a vice. Therefore, she will distribute these gifts with great discretion and prudence, for munificence is one of the things that most magnifies the reputation of great lords and ladies. John of Salisbury proves this in *Polycraticus* (book three, chapter twenty-four) by demonstrating that the virtue of generosity is necessary for those who rule over public affairs. For example, Titus, the noble emperor, acquired such renown through his generosity that he was known as the benefit, the relief and the help of all persons. He loved this virtue of largesse so much that the day he had not given any gift he could not be happy. In this way he acquired the general favour and love of everyone.

The wise lady will demonstrate her generosity like this: if she has the power to give, and she learns that some foreign gentlemen or other people have lost much of their wealth through long imprisonment or ransom or are suffering great penury, she will help them with her own resources very willingly and liberally as a matter of course, according to her ability. As largesse does not consist only in material gifts, as a wise man has said, but also in comforting words, she will comfort them with hopes for a better future. This comfort will perhaps do them as much good as, or even more good than, the money that she gives them, for it is very agreeable to any person when a prince or princess comforts him, even just in words.

If this lady sees any gentleman, be he knight or squire, of good courage who has a great desire to increase his honour but does not have much money to outfit himself properly, and if she sees that it is worth while to help him, the gentle lady will do so, for she has within her all good impulses for honour and gentility and for always encouraging noble and valiant actions. And thus in various situations that may arise this lady will extend wise and well-considered largesse. And if any great lords give her presents or gifts she will reward the messengers so generously that they will have cause to rejoice. She will give more to foreigners than to other people so that in their country they may mention her generosity to their lords. She will want her stewards to deliver the gifts promptly. If great ladies give her presents, she will send them some of her jewels and fine things, but more generously. If a poor or simple person does her any service or kindly presents her with some curiosity, she will consider the abilities of the person and his or her social position and the importance of the service, or the value, beauty or novelty of the gift, according to the case. Whatever the remuneration is, she will give it so abundantly that the person will rejoice. Furthermore, she will receive the thing with such a delighted expression that it will be half the payment by itself.

She will certainly not do what we saw happen once, something that we thought was deplorable at a sophisticated court of a prince or princess. A person was summoned there who was considered wise, so that the court might hear and learn his knowledge. He attended the court several times and everyone felt greatly satisfied with his deeds and his counsel. As a result of his knowledge he did the ruler certain just, good and laudable services that were worthy of commendation and reward. At the same time another person frequented this same court who had the reputation of being a buffoon and was in the habit of entertaining the lords and ladies with jests and stories of what everyone was doing everywhere and with worthless chatter in the way of mockery and jokes. It was decided that they both be remunerated, and so gifts were given both to the person who was reputed to be wise and who had deserved them because of his knowledge and to the person reputed to be a fool who had done nothing but tell his jokes. A gift was given to this buffoon that was valued at forty *écus* and to the other a gift worth twelve *écus*. When we three sisters, Reason, Rectitude and Justice, saw this, we hid our faces with shame at seeing such improper valuation and such blind ignorance in a court that is supposed to be famous. We were ashamed not for the value of the gifts but for the relative esteem for the persons and their deeds. The wise princess will not behave in this way and will not have to do with foolish people or those who imitate the ways of this court. Neither will she have much time for worthless things, nor will she offer her gifts for them, but to the virtuous and to those who have done something worth while.

20. How good princesses who for some reason cannot put the foregoing advice into effect may be excused.

Now we have described the largesse of the wise princess, but so that it may not be forgotten, before we pass on to other matters we should mention here questions that could be asked of us on two points that we have previously touched on: that is, how the wise princess should make herself acquainted with people of all classes among her subjects, and how she ought to be generous, as we said a moment ago. The objections might be phrased: 'You say that it is best for the wise princess to be well regarded by her subjects, and therefore she ought to get to know them, but how may this principle be of use to everyone? Undoubtedly there are many who, although they are very wise and prudent, have bad-tempered husbands who keep them on such a tight rein that they hardly dare speak, even to their servants and to people of their house-hold. As these women are not able to meet anyone, this precept cannot apply to them. As for the other point, there are many princes and other men who similarly keep their wives so short of money that they don't have a penny, and so the wives, as a result, cannot practise this virtue of generosity, even though they may have good will.'

We can easily reply to both these questions in one sentence: that is, that we are not referring to those who are guarded so closely. To the ladies and princesses or others held in such servitude Prudence can give no other teaching (but for all that, it is no small thing) except to endure patiently, always to do good so far as it is in their power, and to obey in order to have peace.

But let us speak to those who we assume have the authority, good sense and power to do what we have said (not counting young women who are still in the charge of other ladies, although if they study our doctrine and understand it, it can help them to learn to govern them-selves with such prudence that when they are of an age of greater discretion, their husbands and lords, who see them so well behaved and so self-disciplined, will be able to give them authority to act and govern on their behalf just as we have advised them and will advise them hereafter). Any man is extremely foolish, of whatever class he may happen to be, if he sees that he has a good and wise wife, yet does not give her authority to govern in an emergency. There are many men who are so churlish and so ignorant that they do not know how to see or recognize goodness and common sense. They cherish the opinion that women are not sensible enough to have much administrative ability, although we often see the opposite of this.

In conclusion, we repeat that if these ladies who are held on such a tight rein cannot put into effect these sensible precepts, both in the matter of getting to know their subjects and also of performing generous acts, they are to be excused. However, just as a bright light cannot be hidden so well that it may not be seen from some angle, neither can their husband hinder them so much that if the ladies are good, wise and loving towards their subjects, they may not be loved by everyone and their good will known. People will see that they are discreet and good, and the ladies will be praised and renowned in all places. And that suffices for this matter.

21. *Of the behaviour of the wise princess who is widowed.*

We have spoken enough about the teachings for married princesses, but so that our doctrine may be valuable to all classes of women we will direct our attention to widowed ladies and princesses, both the young and the elderly. Here is what we have to say: if the prudent princess remains a widow, there is no doubt that she will lament her bereavement, and she will keep herself secluded for a time after the funeral and obsequies, with only a little daylight and in sad and mournful weeds, according to decent custom. She will not forget the good soul of her husband, but will pray for him and have prayers said very carefully and devoutly in Masses, services, chantries, offerings and oblations. She will do everything she can to recommend his soul to all devout people. This remembrance and her good deeds will not last a short time, but for as long as she lives.

Nevertheless, Prudence will say to this very sensible lady (and her confessor and other appropriate people will advise her often) that in spite of her great loss and her great sorrow and regret of the death of her lord, and in spite of the good and loyal love that she bore him, she must be patient with everything that God wills. We are all born to go the same way when it shall please Him. She might easily sin and anger Our Lord by being so grief-stricken for too long a time. She should take up a new way of living, or she could harm her soul and her health, and that would not be good for her noble children, who still need her.

This lady, thus admonished by Reason and Good Advice in order to pass through this great tribulation somewhat better, will begin to give some thought to her own needs. First of all she will want to understand thoroughly the last will and testament of her husband, and she will devote all her efforts to fulfilling his wishes as soon as possible in order to ease the blessed soul of the man she loved. Afterwards, if she has children and the father has not allotted their portions during his lifetime, she will take great care that with advice from the barons and wise counsellors a fair distribution of land and lordships be made among them to the satisfaction of each one. If she can, she will try hard to keep their affection without any disagreement among them. She will try to ensure that all the younger ones serve and honour the eldest, their lord, as is only right. In addition, she will find out what should be coming to her, in the matter of both personal property and her dower. If she has no children and anyone wishes to cheat her out of what belongs to her (as often happens to widowed ladies, be they great or little), she will summon good assistance and will use it to protect and defend her rights boldly by law and reason. She will refrain from using hot and hasty words to anyone, but she will protect her rights; she will state her case or have it stated courteously to everyone. As long as she lives she will greatly cherish the parents of her husband. She will bear great honour to them, and for doing this, she will be greatly praised and esteemed.

But if the princess remains a widow while her eldest son is still young and under age, and by chance war and strife break out among the barons, for the sake of good government she must use her prudence and her knowledge to establish and maintain peace among them. No war against foreign enemies could be so perilous to her as this. Therefore, the lady, being very sensible, and bearing in mind the evil that can come of their antagonisms, and seeing that her son is still small and young, will be such a good mediator between them by her prudent conduct and wisdom that she will find a way to reconcile them. In order to do this she will look for the most suitable strategy, and she will do her best to negotiate with them with kindness and skill, always using good and loyal counsel. Or if some lands rebel, or the country is attacked by foreign enemies (as often happens after the death of a prince with under-age children), and therefore it may be necessary to make and conduct war, the prudent lady and princess who desires to preserve the well-being of her children will certainly need to put into effect her great wisdom. Then it will be necessary for her to keep the good will of the barons and lords so that they are always good and loyal and can be depended upon to come to the aid of her child. Also she must have the affection of the knights, squires and gentlemen, so that they will gladly and boldly fight with greater valour, if it is necessary to prosecute war for their young lord. She must keep the affection of the people too, so that they will the more willingly help her with their wealth and possessions, if need be, to prosecute the war. Therefore, so that they may always be very loyal subjects and others cannot persuade them to betray her, she will often speak to them, saying kindly that she does not wish to vex them; but if they are in any way aggrieved by the great expense of the war and other matters, if it pleases God, this situation will not last very long; she will never forget their goodness and loyalty and will remind her son of it.

The wise lady and princess will speak along these lines to those who can be valuable in this situation, for it will persuade them to give up their money to her more willingly, and it will keep them from rebellion. Rebellions most often happen because the people are too oppressed by lords and ruled with harshness. Beyond a doubt, such a princess can do inestimable good in the kingdom and country.

22. Of the same: advice to young widowed princesses.

If the princess remains a widow without children, and if she wishes to live more comfortably and in peace when she has been awarded her proper dower, she will go to live on her lands. There she will consider how she can manage her affairs well and wisely according to her income. She will immediately summon her principal men and also all the officers and bailiffs of her lordships. She will want to know by thorough inquiry how they are overseen, how they have conducted themselves in the past and whether they are upright men. She will find out what the local customs are. If those officers are good, they will stay where they are, but if they are bad, she will dismiss them and replace them with new men who have been recommended to her. She will certainly not want her offices to be sold to the highest bidder, as is commonly done now in France. In many places there are devourers of poor people, wicked debauchers and worse than thieves, for there is no wickedness that they will not stoop to for money, and in all truth, the common experience verifies it. But the good lady who knows about the situation and has considered the matter will not want these offices of hers to be bought or sold, but rather awarded to the wisest and most deserving men, as is proper. They must particularly see to it that justice is well observed, or otherwise she will remove them and punish them. And it will be expressly forbidden to the people of her household, as well as her officers, to dare to injure any of her subjects or to take anything without paying for it. She will not want the property of the poor to weigh heavy on her soul, and therefore she will have full knowledge of the great extortions that the buyers for lords and ladies often perpetrate upon the common people. If the lords and ladies do not prevent these extortions, they will not be excused in the eyes of God, for they ought to know about them and not permit them. She will want her officers and servants to keep the peace and resist all evil as best they can. In brief, she will keep their affection, and she will want them and their wives to visit her often, and she will make them welcome. Both townswomen and well-born ladies and maidens of the country will come to her, and she will receive them with pleasure, honouring each one according to her right. She will summon them to accompany her when lords or strangers wish to visit her. Even the common women of the village, who will love this noble lady with all their heart, will bring her their little gifts, like fruit, or other things. She will have them come to visit her; she will want to see them and receive their trinkets with pleasure. She will make much of even a trifle and say that there is nothing else so good nor so fine. She will thank them warmly; she will speak with them about their families and their households. As a result, when the women go back to their homes, they will make a great celebration and subject for conversation of the welcome that their lady made them, considering themselves greatly honoured because of it, and they will chatter about it endlessly with their neighbours.

This noble lady will not think it beneath her to visit women in childbed, both rich and poor. She will give to the poor for the love of God, and she will honour the rich. She will be godmother to their children, and in short, she will conduct herself so charitably in every way and show herself to be so kind and humane towards her subjects that they will talk of nothing but her. They will pray for her, and they will love her with all their heart. The most noble widowed queens and princesses of France whom I have named above knew very well how to conduct themselves in this way. That is, Queen Jeanne, Queen Blanche, the Duchess of Orleans (the daughter of King Charles IV), and likewise others who conduct themselves according to such goodness and wisdom that they may always be examples of good and wise living to those women who come later.

This is the end of the instruction that Prudence gives the wise princess who is of an age to know the difference between right and wrong. After that introduction, we will now say a little something first about the young widowed princess and then about young married ladies.

As long as the young princess remains a widow, it is best that she be under the guidance of her parents, obey their wishes, and be governed entirely by them and by their regulations, nor should she undertake anything without their knowledge and permission. She ought to dress simply according to the style of clothing of the country where she lives and be modest and demure both in appearance and in behaviour.

Games that are too merry, all dances, tight gowns, and all frivolity are forbidden to her. And even if she is fun-loving by nature and her youth prompts her to laugh, play and sing, it is imperative, if she wishes to preserve her honour, that she renounce these activities, at least if she is not in private, and she should never indulge in them in front of men. Especially among lords and ladies or strange knights or other gentlemen, she should behave very prudently, have a composed expression when speaking, and look about her without putting on airs. Then people will say that it is an excellent thing for such a young lady to have such fine deportment and such a dignified expression. It is not at all seemly for her to speak or confer privately with men, whoever they may be, nor for knights, squires, nor other men to be in her company too much without a reasonable excuse, and they should never be in her chamber. For such things can soon cause a few words to slip out, even with little foundation, and her character can be besmirched and fall into disrepute. The principal lady who has charge of her ought to be very watchful of this danger, but to avoid boredom and idleness the young widow ought to amuse herself at festivals and play five-stones with her women, and other simple and decorous games. On weekdays she should keep herself occupied with useful employment.

The young widow should be particularly careful not to say anything about marriage to any person privately, in secret or without the knowledge of her friends, nor should she listen to any talk about it if someone wants to bring up the subject, for such discussions would do her no credit and she could well be deceived. She ought to pay close attention to her friends in the matter of remarriage and take care to do nothing about it without them, for if she married by her own choice without their wholehearted consent, she would be greatly at fault. If she made a bad match and no good came of it, no one would ever feel sorry for her and she would lose her friends' favour. She ought to bear in mind that they probably know better how to recognize what is good for her than she herself does.

23. Of the behaviour that ought to be instilled into a young newly married princess.

We began earlier by explaining how the wise princess arranges for her daughters to be brought up and instructed in childhood and youth. In continuing this matter, we must now describe the proper system for the daughter of a prince, that is, the young princess who wishes to live according to the rules of propriety after she is married and out of the jurisdiction of her parents.

We say: the young newly married princess must acquire men and women servants of such calibre as is in keeping with the exalted position of the prince and lord to whom she has been given in marriage. Gentlemen will be chosen to be her servants, not too young nor too talkative nor gallant, but sensible and moderate and men of merit. If they are married, so much the better, especially those who are going to serve her at table and who will be most in the company of her and her women. It would be seemly for their wives also to live at court, if possible. The masters of the household should be mature and capable persons so that they may be good teachers and guides for the young princess. As for her conscience and the salvation of her soul, a wise religious confessor ought to be chosen for her: a scholar in divinity, prudent in manners, a man of native intelligence, a worthy and upright man who leads a good life.

As for her women, since older ladies and maidens as well as young ones will be employed at her court, she must find out such things about them as whether they are sensible and what their social position is and what sort of life they lead and have led before they are given a place at court. They should be examined in much greater detail than would be necessary for the women at the court of an older princess, although in all courts it is most seemly that the women there have high moral standards. Greater peril may be present in the retinue of a young princess than in that of an older one for two particular reasons.

The first reason is that one commonly judges the quality and status of the lord or the lady by the conditions and conduct that one sees in the household, so that if the women did not behave well, some could suppose that the mistress did not either, and the lady's honour could suffer. The second reason is that this young and childlike mistress could be influenced by the unsuitable example of some of her women. She ought to have a lady or maiden of a mature age – wise, prudent, good, virtuous and devout – who may be confidently entrusted with the chaperonage of the young lady. Even if there are many ladies of better lineage and parentage at the court in the retinue of this princess who might also be honourable companions, this older lady will nevertheless have the care and the principal responsibility for her. If she really wants to do her duty, this lady will have no small responsibility and no little care, for she must attend to two principal matters.

The first is that she establish and maintain her mistress in wise conduct and high moral standards, such that no voices may be raised nor words spread against her honour. The other is that she gain the affection of her mistress and always have her favour. Accomplishing these two things (that is, to give correction and teaching to young people and to have both their love and their favour) is often a very difficult business. She must go about it with great discretion, and she can do this in the following way.

It is a very much more difficult thing to put out a fire when it has ignited and engulfed a house than to see to it that it never gets started. Therefore, the wise housewife, constantly on her guard to avoid any possible danger, often checks over the house, especially in the evening, for fear that some careless servant may have left a candle or wick or something else lying around that might prove dangerous. In just the same way a young lady's chaperon, considering what she will have to do in the way of bending the twig when it is young, will want to try as best she can to bend her mistress in such a way that she may ever after remain so. Therefore, gradually and not suddenly, lest the twig snap, she will seek the means to attain her ends and the desired result. First of all, with a gracious and courteous manner, and by giving her some little trinkets that please young people, she will take infinite pains to show that she is amiable in order to have the love of her young mistress. Sometimes, in games or amusements when they are off by themselves and in private, just like two young people together, the good lady, although she may be of mature years or even elderly, will sometimes tell fables and stories of the sort that one tells children. She will do all this to win over her mistress, so that she may accept it more willingly when she must reprimand and correct her, for if she always displayed a solemn manner without laughter and without games, youth, which is inclined to merriment and diversions, would not be able to tolerate her. The young lady would fear and dislike her and would not take her corrections kindly. When the chaperon sees that she is in her mistress's good graces, and that the young lady feels quite affectionate towards her, then according to the maturity or the emotion that she perceives in her, when they are in their chambers she will acquaint her with certain stories about ladies and maidens who conducted themselves very well, and how they were well received and gained honour by it, and conversely, how trouble followed those who conducted themselves foolishly. She will say that she saw it happen in her time, and above all she will make the stories lively and interesting. She will add that she does not tell these stories for any other reason but to entertain her with their adventures. She will learn how to tell stories so interestingly that she will move the hearts of her mistress and others who hear her, all gathered around her eagerly listening to her. She will sometimes tell stories of both men and women saints, their lives and sufferings, and sometimes, so that the conversation does not get tiresome, she will intersperse some humorous trifle, and likewise will want the others to speak so that each one tells a story in her turn.

The wise lady will use these devices in winning over the young princess to love her. As for correction and teaching, by courteous and choice words she will suggest that the young lady get up quite early. She will teach her some brief but good prayers, and will exhort her to recite them as she gets up. First salute Our Lord and the Blessed Virgin. She will say that she has heard that no one who has the habit of heartily addressing her first words on rising to Our Lord will have any misfortune during the day, and in this she will be telling the truth, for many people have this custom and it is a very good one. She will have her mistress groomed and dressed properly without taking so long about it as a good many ladies do, which is a great waste of time and a bad habit. She will have her go to Mass and say her prayers devoutly and carefully, and moreover she will encourage all the good conduct and speech, bearing, ornaments and clothing that are proper to a princess of noble birth. She will counsel her to behave and conduct herself irreproachably. And, to be brief, by her wise admonitions the older lady will finally get her to the point where everyone will say that considering her tender years they have never seen a lady with such deportment nor one better taught. People will say of her, 'This young heart deserves great praise for being old and mature through good manners! Truly I suppose that this young lady is of such a high calibre that she is eager to be instructed and wishes to remember everything she has learned.'

However, the girl might be so perverse that the lady would be excused if she could not instruct her or discipline her. The lady should bring to bear the following pressure when she reprimands her mistress for some fault of the sort young people commit. Even though the girl is good and meek and she has her under firm control, if she behaves otherwise or continues to do something wrong, or says certain things, the lady will threaten to leave her and go back to her home and never serve her again. She will say that carrying on in this way is neither nice nor proper for a lady like her. If the young princess is good and meek and loves the lady, she will be afraid that she may leave her and will therefore mend her ways with very few threats. But if the girl is surly and malicious, spiteful and aloof, she will tell her privately and quite frankly that she must understand, whether she likes it or not, that she will tell her parents and friends, or her husband if need be, if she does not behave herself differently.

Although this lady has the responsibility of teaching her young mistress proper behaviour, she will nevertheless be tolerant. She will understand that it is natural for youth to play and laugh, and so she will set aside a time and a place for it for the young lady and the younger women among her servants, and she will ensure that there are no outsiders in the vicinity. She will assume that her mistress will not get up to mischief, for one cannot and should not oversee all the young people's pleasures, provided that they are not unseemly or improper.

We will not speak any further now on this subject of the manners and deportment appropriate to well-disciplined youth, because it will be mentioned later in the letter that the elderly lady may send to her mistress.

24. How the wise lady or maiden lady who has charge of a young princess ought to maintain the good reputation of her mistress and the love of her husband.

As youth accustomed to a life of pleasure sometimes can be easily inclined to too much gaiety, the lady must be able to steer the young person who is not too obstinate back onto the right track. She must be especially careful to nip situations in the bud lest something regrettable should happen (we have touched upon this before). The following are some possible tactics.

Having the young princess under her tutelage and seeing the love between the prince her lord and her mistress, such as young newly married people have for each other, the wise lady will make every possible effort to nurture them in this love. She will advise them always to say sweet and loving words and to do things to please each other.

She will take pains to carry affectionate messages and nice gifts between them herself. She will always convey commendations and greetings to promote peace and love between them, and she will see to it that anything to the contrary is prevented and avoided. And privately, when the lord is not there and the young princess retires to bed, the older lady will engage her in conversation about him, reminding her of the good words that she has often heard him say of his love for her, and she will tell her how good and handsome and gracious he is, and all sorts of similar things.

As it is customary that lords, knights, squires and other strangers sometimes come near the princesses and ladies, and their lords and even parents encourage it, the ladies must see and speak to many people. They must entertain them appropriately in feasts and sometimes dances or in conversation or other diversions, according to the case. Now it sometimes happens that some of the men at such gatherings are bowled over with love for ladies, or anyway wish to give the impression that they are. Therefore the wise chaperon, who will always be near her mistress, will watch the appearance and manner of everyone attentively to see if she can perceive any sign that anyone may be getting these ideas. If she thinks she has noticed something, she will say nothing about it to anyone, but rather will keep it a secret in her own mind. And when everyone has departed and the party is over and her mistress has withdrawn, it may happen (if her mistress is a close friend of hers) that she herself will start the conversation with her chaperon, saying, 'Didn't we dance tonight!' This man and that one are charming, or they are not, or something else. And then the wise lady can reply in words like these: 'I don't know, but I didn't see anyone who seemed to me so kind nor so handsome and charming as my lord, and I had a good look around. I think that compared to the others he is the best favoured in all respects.'

But if the lord is old or ugly she will say: 'To tell the truth, I hardly noticed anyone else in the company except my lord, for compared to the others he seemed so clearly the lord and prince. And how good it is to hear him speak, for he speaks so wisely!' But let us suppose that this has not been the case: she will still recall something about him that she can praise, but she will say nothing about what she may really think.

The chaperon will watch carefully to see whether one or more of the men whom she suspected go out of their way to be in the company of her mistress and whether they are looking for ways and means of getting to know her or her parents or anyone else who could introduce them to her, or whether they or any of their companions try to get acquainted with any of her women. If she sees that after this feast or gathering none of the men whom she had suspected makes any such attempt in any way as far as she can see, she will forget about it and abandon her suspicions. But if she perceives those signs or similar ones, she will set to work to remedy the situation and do her duty, although her heart may be full of great care and worry. She must work very cautiously; if she is wise and prudent she will keep from revealing the situation to anyone, for it would be a very bad thing to do.

But what is she to do for the best and how is she to go about her task most wisely? When she is sure that someone is diligently trying to win the love of her mistress, before he has had a chance to say anything to her about it (always supposing that he would be so bold as to declare himself to her), the chaperon will give him such a warm welcome that he will have the chance to get acquainted with her. He will seize this opportunity, for he will think that because she is the closest one to the young lady, his petition ought to carry all the more weight. Before long he will be emboldened to tell her what he has in his heart and make great pledges of services and all the favours that he will do for her, according to the custom of men in these circumstances. Then the lady will be ready with her reply and will speak to him as briefly as possible and without the knowledge of her mistress. She will reply to him quietly and fearlessly in these words, if they are appropriate in the circumstances.

She will say to him: 'Sir, truly it has not escaped my notice by your manner that you have had in mind what you have told me, but I wanted the words to come from you. I first desired to have this acquaintance with you so that you could tell me about it and I might know it before anyone else who might report the thing and reveal the secret. I am quite pleased that I have at present decided to make you this reply about what you have told me, as it reflects my firm resolve, which, upon my life, I promise to God and to you, will never change. Without making you a very long sermon about this or going on at too great a length, I tell you quite briefly and once and for all, that so long as I am living and in her company, this young lady (who, by the confidence that her friends and her lord have in me, although I am unworthy of so much, is entrusted to my care) will do no wrong.

Nor will she do anything that would give rise to reproaches or any talk other than what is proper about a lady like her of the noble blood from which she is descended. With the help of God I certainly intend to prevent it, although her virtue is easy to protect, for I know quite well that all her love is reserved for her husband, just as it ought to be. I know that she is altogether good and of a high moral character and that she would not have anything to do with an illicit love affair nor even think of it. And I know her so well that if you or anyone else said anything to her or if she noticed something, I know she would hate above all else the man who she thought had in mind any such thing in regard to her.

'I beg of you, Sir, with all my heart, please abandon the whole idea and think no more about it, for I swear to you by my Christianity that you are wasting your time. Just so that you have no false hopes, I swear on my soul to you that, supposing that she did wish it (which I know very well that she would never do), I would put so many obstacles in the way of it that a love affair would be impossible. Believe me, and do not make any more such attempts, for upon my soul I will not allow them! I would be obliged to tell certain persons who would not thank you for this and who would keep her out of your clutches. I have but one death to die, and I would prefer it rather than that I should consent to or see the dishonour of my mistress. It is best that this business never be mentioned again and that we leave it at that.'

The wise lady will make this reply or one like it, and she will not change her attitude for a promise, gift, offer, or threat, nor can he do anything either then or at another time that may sway her to the contrary. She will be very careful not to have a changed or fiery expression, nor angry eyes when she parts from him, but rather she will have a composed expression and an assured manner, as though they had been talking about something else, so that no one could infer the real subject from seeing them together. Also the lady will take care that no word gets out about it to her mistress nor to anyone else, even an intimate friend, nor will she ever give any sign of it, not even the least hint. She will be very careful that none of her women or servants, or anyone else, whispers to her mistress in a way that may suggest such a thing, for she will immediately notice it in their manner of laughing and speaking. Let us suppose that she does not hear them, but if she definitely does notice something of the kind, she will not keep quiet about it, but rather will threaten the person with dismissal if she takes it upon herself to whisper to her mistress any more, for it is not seemly. And so she will keep a close watch that nobody has the opportunity of making any report to the young lady.

It may happen that this young man nevertheless cannot restrain himself and will come and go by some sly means that he will have found with the help of an accomplice and by which now and then he can visit the place. The chaperon cannot very well prevent this, for if she mentioned it, very great evil could come of it, so she will refrain from doing so, and she will watch her lady and mistress closely. But if she cannot watch her closely enough to prevent her mistress from noticing, or seeing by signs or veiled words, that this fellow will tell his intention and desire, she will still not be afraid of anything, because she will know quite well that many ladies and maidens are loved and cajoled who are, however, very little interested and do not love their suitors. Still, she will be very careful to see whether the young lady or princess takes any pleasure in his company. She will note whether she talks about him more readily than about another, or if her face lights up when she sees him or if her expression changes at all. When they are alone together she will try her best with gracious and kind words to draw her out about what she has in her heart for this man and whether he has mentioned his feelings to her. And then, according to what she says or confesses, the chaperon can reply to her.

If the young lady says that truly she has seen it or that he has told her and that she is very troubled and angered by it and that it grieves her very much, the chaperon, who will be wise and discerning, will take good note of her words. She will want to make inquiries of her very prudently and tactfully without showing herself in the beginning too antagonistic. On the one hand, the chaperon will want to speak diffidently to give the young lady the impression that she is not giving it much thought, but on the other hand she will want to speak her mind with great conviction. If in the end the young lady declares that she does not intend to encourage the man, the chaperon will be very happy and she will urge her with all her might to keep her good resolution. She will give her many examples of the evil that can happen and that often has happened to many women through such follies, the great dishonour and reproach that spring from them, and the deceit that is in men. She will urge her to be careful to respond wisely to this fellow every time he talks to her and to tell him quite

93

briefly that he is wasting his time and tell him in the strongest terms that never, for all his persuasion, will he change her mind; he is annoying her with such talk, she is not interested in the looks he gives her, and furthermore she rejects him and sends him away in no uncertain terms. The chaperon will urge her to be very careful that she does not, by any look in her eyes, or by speech, smile or manner, give any indication to him by which she may lead him on or raise his hopes.

The chaperon will teach her the manner that she ought to adopt to get rid of him courteously. When he comes, she will have someone tell him that she is resting or that she is busy with something and she hopes he will not be offended that she cannot see him this time. When she has had him told this sort of thing several times and continues to take such an attitude over a long period, he may at last realize that he would be wasting his time to keep trying. Moreover, the noble lady will strongly urge her mistress to be very careful not to mention this thing to either man or woman, for evil could result from it. It is the greatest common sense to keep quiet about it, and it does no honour to a woman to brag about such a thing. She will forbid her to mention it, for if she does, she might speak to someone who would not give her good advice, but rather would perhaps encourage her and plunge her into folly, or who would not conceal the affair very well. In this way some whiff of it could get out and evil result. And so by this prudent course the good lady will finally extinguish and crush this whole business, regardless of who may hate her for it or feel resentful. The person who may feel such hatred will not disturb her in any way, and she will not in the least fear anyone when her 'offence' has been to do good, for the one who hates her for it in the very beginning will love her for it in the end. The young lady will esteem her a thousand times more when she recognizes her great prudence and her constant goodness, for a good deed is always valuable eventually. She will be the cause for this young princess's being in her time a very wise, good and virtuous lady, and having the excellent qualities that we have described.

25. Of the young high-born lady who wants to plunge into a foolish love affair, and the instruction that Prudence gives to her chaperon.

As people are not all the same, there are some men and women so perverse that whatever good correction and instruction they are given, they will always follow their own wicked inclinations. It is fruitless to show them the error of their ways, and nothing is gained but their resentment. We will now describe the instruction of the good lady who has in her charge and control some young princess or lady and the attitude that she ought to adopt in the event that she should see her mistress go astray in a foolish love affair and refuse her wise and good advice.

If it happens that some young princess or high-born lady is so lacking in knowledge or constancy that she is unable, does not know how, or does not wish to resist the appeals of the man who is trying his best to attract her by various signs and gestures (as men well know how to do in such a case), and that the lady who has charge of her perceives by these signs and gestures that the girl is attracted to him, whatever she may say to deny it, the chaperon will deplore this state of affairs with all her heart. But in spite of some natural aversion to it, she will do her duty of admonishing her for her own good. The older lady will not keep her concern to herself nor will she hesitate to take the girl aside and tell her gently at first and then with dire warnings. And if she sees the young woman continue, she must show her the great evil and danger and the very great damage that can come of it, and without ceasing from this she will persuade her, perhaps enough to put a stop to the business. By having serious talks with her, the chaperon may be able to make her renounce this idea before the foolishness gets any further advanced.

But it may happen that nothing she says has any effect. The chaperon may see her taking advice privately from some of her other women who, she may suspect, know of her disposition and intention. The chaperon will try her best to warn her about the miseries that will result, but the proud and spirited girl may be aloof towards her chaperon and show in various ways that she may not wish to defer to her any longer. It may seem to the young woman that she is no longer a child to be under the chaperon's control and subject to her correction. She may not take criticism with a good grace; she may

95

reply haughtily, half threateningly, and frown and snap at the chaperon. The older lady will realize from this that she is in disfavour with her and that she would like to be free of her the better to do as she pleases. And perhaps the lady will hear that she sometimes says privately to some of her young attendants, who will be more in favour with her, 'The devil take the old bat! What a sourpuss! We're stuck with her until she fries in Hell!' And another will reply, 'So help me God, Madam, you should scatter peas on the steps so that she'll break her neck!' And so on and so forth.

What will the wise lady do now when she sees that there is no remedy? She has done her duty and assuaged her conscience by having explained the situation to the girl and having got her confessor to tell her the evils that could come to her for committing this folly. But her mistress is so besotted that nothing can be done about it, and she has already found a way of doing what she wants willy-nilly and regardless of whom it might displease. It is impossible to protect someone who does not wish to be protected from herself. People are already beginning to talk about her and notice her. Even among her attendants there may be certain young women who, being envious and knowing something of the young lady's secret, are the favourites and hear bits of gossip and may do a great disservice to her.

Now even though her heart may be extraordinarily heavy about it, she as a prudent lady will ponder the best course of action, considering the evil and peril that could come to her herself from this thing if she remains any longer at court. For suppose that she was not a party to the deed (which she would not countenance if her life depended on it), and the thing got to be known, whether by the young woman's parents or her husband, the chaperon would get all the blame for it. They would say, 'Why didn't you tell us about it? We would have put a stop to it! We were counting on you to let us know.' But she would not mention this situation for anything because of the perils and evils that could ensue from it. For whoever has a conscience and common sense ought indeed to dread making a report of such things to the husband or to friends or to anyone at all. The chaperon cannot remain there any longer without running the risk of one other great danger that could come to her through the hatred of her mistress or of the one who is wooing her, because they would fear and distrust her somewhat and look upon her as an obstacle.

Therefore she, who will be in all things circumspect, will now need to use prudently her great knowledge and skill. She will keep absolutely quiet about this thing; she will no longer speak either good or evil to her lady and mistress. She will not make any expression or any sign which may displease the young lady, but as soon as she can by some good method (which she will already have long since devised the moment that she first saw the situation of her mistress change) she will depart from court with the good will of the lord if she can, but if she is good and wise she will take good care that he cannot suspect the real reason that she wishes to leave. If she knows that he wishes to retain her, she will think of some reason to serve the purpose, either illness or old age, or some serious physical disability. If he wishes to inquire too much into the cause of her departure before he gives her permission to leave, she will say that she has some illness and should not be in contact with the young lady until she recovers from it; and thus she will excuse herself.

But it may happen that her mistress herself, seeing that her chaperon has stopped harping about her conduct, will be sorry to see her go. This is because the girl will think that she would get away with doing as she pleased as long as she was with this chaperon, for people would not be so quick to talk if she was accompanied by such a lady. She will try to flatter her and make promises to her so that she will stay, but the good lady will know how to excuse herself well and wisely from this, saying that she is truly ill, but that when she is well again she will certainly be able to come back. Although her heart may be sick at leaving and she may feel tenderness for her mistress, if she is wise she will certainly be on her guard against staying on, for whatever blandishments, or later she will regret it.

But if it happens that the lady is happy about her departure, when she comes to take her leave, she will speak to the girl privately on bended knee, thanking her humbly for the gifts and honours that she has bestowed upon her, and begging her to pardon her. If she has done or said anything displeasing to her, she did it out of the great love and concern that she felt for her mistress, for she tried to do her duty well and properly, as was befitting to her mistress's rank. It makes her quite ill to leave her, but she is old and weak and can no longer do her job properly. Or perhaps old age makes her so grumpy and so bad-tempered that she cannot manage to keep up with the lively doings of the young people as well as she ought to. And so she prefers to leave and hopes it may be with her blessing. She beseeches her that she may leave with all her good will, for of this much she can be quite certain, that never in her life will she have a servant who loves her and her honour better or more loyally than she does and always will do all her life.

On her departure the lady will say this kind of thing to her mistress, who, out of the joy she feels at her departure, will perhaps reply to her with charming speeches. Or perhaps the older lady has had charge of her for a long time, perhaps since childhood, and it will make the young woman's heart heavy. The young woman will perhaps say to her that she bears her no resentment for anything except what she has made known to her, which she has never held against her, and such kinds of appeals. To these things the lady, who will not wish to argue with her because she knows very well that nothing will persuade her, will reply that it may indeed have happened that in her zeal caused by the great apprehension that she felt for her she had had some suspicions. The chaperon will beg her to please pardon her everything, saying that she may be certain that never in her life would she breathe a word to anyone about any suspicion that she may have had, nor what it may have been about, nor did she ever do so, except to her for her own good. And so saying, she will depart.

The letter that is contained in the *Book of the Duke of True Lovers**
and that Sybil de la Tour sent to the Duchess can serve the purpose and is reproduced in the next chapter. Whoever wishes can pass over it, or read it, or leave it if she has seen it before, although it is good and profitable to hear and take note of for all ladies and any others who may find it useful.

26. An example of the sort of letter the wise lady may send to her mistress.

It may happen after all this that the young lady will behave with such bad judgement after the departure of her former chaperon that gossip will arise detrimental to her honour. It may increase so much that this good lady who had charge of her and now lives at her own home will hear about it, and it will make her very sad to see the honour of her mistress diminish, when she has taken so many pains to instruct her as well as she possibly could. She will not know what to do about the outcome of this business. When she has thought a good deal about this matter, regardless of the gratitude or lack of it that the young

---

* *Le Livre du duc des vrais amants* by Christine de Pisan, *ca.* 1401.

lady may show her, she will be compelled by great love to write to her and recapitulate the warnings that she used to give her in case she might be able to benefit her after all, because what is written down is sometimes better remembered and penetrates the heart more than what is said orally. She will write these or similar words in a letter, or she will dictate them to a priest very secretly in confession. Then she will have the priest deliver the letter.

'My most respected lady and mistress, I earnestly and humbly recommend myself to you. May it please you not to bear me any ill will if I am now compelled by great love to write to you for your own good, although, my most respected lady, I realize that I am scarcely in a position to lecture you about your own good, as if you were still in my care, as you were since childhood until now (although I was not worthy of it). It seems to me that I would be wrong to keep silent about what I know could set you on a course for sorrow if I did not alert you to it. Therefore, dear lady, I am writing to you in this letter what follows, and I again beg you very humbly not to bear me any ill will for it, for you can be quite sure that I am prompted by very great love and a desire for your noble renown and honour to increase.

'My lady, news of your behaviour has reached me, and I grieve about it with all my heart, for I fear the decline of your good reputation. Just as any princess or high-born lady is raised high in honour and position above others, it seems to me right and reasonable that she ought to surpass all other ladies in good prudence, moral standards, conduct and manners, so that she may be an example on which other ladies (and for that matter all women) ought to model themselves in all their actions. She should worship God devoutly. She should have a confident bearing, calm and serene, be moderate and quiet in her diversions, laugh softly and not without cause, have a dignified manner, a humble expression, and good posture. She should respond to everyone kindly and be amiable in speech; her clothing and ornaments should be fine, but not too elaborate. She speaks with authority to strangers, welcoming them, not being overly familiar, and listening to them and not letting her attention wander. At no time does she appear mean, cruel or scornful, nor is she too strict with her women and servants. She should be humane and approachable, not too haughty, and generous within reason in giving gifts. She should know how to recognize the best of her servants and those who are most worthy in goodness and bravery; she should cultivate them and reward them according to their merits. She should neither believe nor trust in flatterers, but recognize them for what they are and send them packing. She should not easily believe hearsay, nor get into the habit of whispering privately in secluded places, even to any of her own people or her women, so that no one can surmise that she is more intimate with one than another. She must not say in front of people to anyone whomsoever veiled words that not everyone understands, so that the hearers do not infer any secret impropriety between them. She ought not to keep herself too shut up in her chamber nor too solitary, nor yet too much in the public view, but at a certain hour she should withdraw, subject to minor variations.

'Although this conduct and all other behaviour appropriate to a great princess were yours formerly, you are at present, it is said, quite changed, for you have become very much more abandoned, more talkative and merrier than you used to be, and that is the kind of thing that usually causes people to have a shrewd idea. Hearts change when the manner changes. Now you want to be alone and withdraw from people except one or two of your women, or some of your servants, to whom you whisper and laugh (even in front of other people) and say veiled words as if you understood each other well, and nothing pleases you except their company, nor can anyone else find favour with you. All these things are the reason your other servants dislike you and suspect that your heart may be smitten with love.

'Oh, my most respected lady, in God's name be careful! You who are at the height where God has raised you, please do not forget your soul and your honour for any empty pleasure. Do not trust in vain thoughts, which many young women have, who persuade themselves that it is not wrong to take a lover provided that there is no wickedness (for I feel certain that otherwise you would never consider doing so), for a lady is happier with a lover and she can make a man valiant and renowned forever. Oh, my dear lady, it is quite otherwise! For the love of God, do not deceive yourself about this nor allow yourself to be deceived! Take a lesson from such great ladies as you have seen in your time who, for merely being suspected of such love without the truth of it ever being proved, lost their honour and their lives from it, for there were such ladies. I swear on my soul that there was no sin, nor guilt, nor wickedness, but yet you have seen their children reproached and held in less esteem because of it. Although for any woman (be she rich or poor) such foolish love is dishonourable, it is all the more improper and harmful in a princess or great lady, the greater she is. There is a good reason for that, for the name of a princess is known by everyone, so that if there is anything disreputable about her, more is known about her in other districts than about ordinary women. Another good reason is their children, who must govern lands and be princes over other people. It is a great misfortune when there is any suspicion that they are not legitimate heirs, and much mischief can come of it.

'Now let us suppose that there is no physical wrongdoing; but those who only hear tell that such-and-such a lady is very much love-smitten will not believe it. For a little apparent vice, perhaps owing to youth, and without wrongdoing, evil tongues will judge her and add things to the story that were never done or thought. And thus such talk, going from mouth to mouth, increases rather than decreases. It is therefore necessary for every great lady to devote greater attention to the details of her manner, behaviour and speech than for other women. The reason is this: when a person comes into the presence of a high-born lady, he directs his gaze at her and his ear to hear what she will say and his understanding to note all her actions. Thus the lady cannot blink, say a word, laugh or make a sign to anyone without everything being noticed and remembered by many people and then reported in various places. When a lady becomes more lively and gay than she used to be and wants to hear more stories about love, and then when her mood changes for any reason, and she suddenly becomes bad-tempered, spiteful and quarrelsome and no one can serve her to her satisfaction and she gets careless about her clothes and her grooming, *then*, of course, people say that she used to be in love, but that she is no longer.

'Don't you think, dearest lady, that this is regrettable behaviour for a great lady, or indeed for any woman? My lady, this is not the manner that a lady ought to have, for she ought to take care, regardless of what she is thinking, that her behaviour and manner are always such that these surmises cannot be made about her, although it can well be difficult to maintain such level-headedness in one's love life. For this reason the safest thing of all is to avoid and flee these situations. You can see, dear lady, that all great ladies, and likewise all women, very much ought to covet a good reputation more than any other treasure whatsoever, for it makes them shine with honour and always remains with them and their children, revered lady, as I have mentioned before. I daresay the arguments that can incline the young lady to love, pleasures and gaiety make her think, "You are young and nothing matters but your pleasure. You can easily love without any wrongdoing. It is not wrong, since there is no sin, and you will make a man valiant. No one will know anything about it, you will live more happily for it, and you will have acquired a true servant and loyal friend," and so on and so forth.

'Oh, my lady, for God's sake do not be deceived by such mad ideas! As for pleasure, you may be certain that in love there is twice as much sorrow, pain, and perilous danger (especially on the side of the ladies) than there is pleasure. Furthermore, love gives rise to many different kinds of bitterness: the fear of losing honour and of being discovered lurks in ladies' hearts, which makes them pay dearly for such pleasures. And as for saying that it will not be wrong since there is no act of sin – alas, Madam, neither men nor women may be so sure of themselves that they can be certain always to love in moderation and prevent the affair from becoming known, as I have said before. Indeed it is impossible, for there is no fire without smoke, although there is quite often smoke without fire. And as for saying, "I will make a man of him" – I say that it is assuredly a very great folly to destroy oneself in order to advance another. Let us suppose that he does become manly by it: this woman indeed destroys herself, when in order to raise another she dishonours herself. And as for saying, "I will have acquired a true friend and servant" – by Heaven, what good could this kind of friend do the lady? For if she was in some difficulty, he would never dare intercede on her behalf for fear of her dishonour. How then will this kind of servant be able to serve her when he will not dare exert himself in her cause? There are some men who say that they serve their ladies when they do many things, be it in arms or other deeds. But I say that they are serving only themselves, for the honour and the benefit remain with them and not with the lady. Still, my lady, you (or anyone else) may wish to excuse yourself, saying, "I have been unlucky in my husband, who is unfaithful and gives me little pleasure. So without doing wrong I can amuse myself with some other man in order to forget melancholy and pass the time." But certainly, with all due respect to your good reverence and to all others who say this, such excuses are worthless. The person who sets fire to his own house in order to burn down his neighbour's commits a very great folly! If this lady who has such a husband bears with him patiently without compromising herself, her honour and the merit of her soul increase all the more.

'As for enjoying herself: certainly, if a great lady and mistress (truly any woman) wishes, she can find enough good, permissible amusements to which she can devote herself and pass the time without melancholy and without this kind of love affair. As for those ladies who have children, what more gracious and delightful pleasure can one ask for than to see them often, to take care that they be well bred and well taught as is appropriate to their high estate? What is more pleasant for a lady than to train her daughters in such a way that in childhood they may adopt a rule for living well and properly by following her example and being in good company? Alas, if the mother was not very prudent, what example would she be to the daughters and to those women who do not have children? Certainly this would not be honourable for any great lady. After she has said her devotions very reverently, she ought to avoid idleness by setting about doing some work or task; she could have fine linens made or silk clothing or something else that she can justly and reasonably use. Such occupations are very good and prevent one from thinking vain things. I do not say that a great lady may not be able to enjoy herself, to laugh and play at a time and place even where there are lords and gentlemen, or that she ought not to honour strangers according to what is appropriate to their dignity, each according to his degree. But this ought to be done so serenely and with such an excellent bearing that there is not a single look nor smile nor word that is not entirely moderate and reasonable. She must always and forever be on her guard that no one may perceive in a word or look or attitude of hers anything unseemly or unbecoming. O God, if all great ladies (and indeed all women) only knew how becoming good manners are in them, they would put more effort into having them than some other adornment, for there is no precious jewel that can adorn a lady so well!

'Finally, my most revered lady, let us turn again to the countless perils and dangers attendant upon this kind of love affair. The first and greatest is that it grieves God. Secondly, if the husband or her parents find out about it, the woman is utterly disgraced, nor will her reputation ever recover. Then again, even if that never happens, we say, in regard to lovers, that although they are all supposedly faithful, discreet and truthful, they are not. On the contrary, one knows many of them who are false. To deceive ladies they say what they neither want nor intend to do. It is invariably true that the intensity of such love does not last long, even among the most faithful; you may be perfectly certain of that. Oh, dear lady, just imagine when this love affair is over and the lady who has been overwhelmed by foolish pleasures regrets them bitterly and reflects on the follies and various perils in which she has often found herself. How much she would wish that she had passed him by and that this had never happened to her and that no one could speak so reproachfully of her! You can never imagine the great repentance and remorse that remain in her heart. Moreover, you and all the others can see what folly it is to put one's body and one's honour at the mercy of the tongues and in the hands of such "servants" (for they are called servants), for in the end the "service" is usually such that although they have promised you and sworn to keep the affair secret, they cannot keep their mouths shut. At the end of such a love affair the ladies are often left to face the blame and common gossip, or at the very least the fear and dread in their hearts, because those very same men whom they trusted, or some other men who know about the affair, talk about it and boast about it. And in this way the ladies in question have abandoned their freedom for servitude and have seen the last of the "service" of this love affair. Consider, Madam, that as it seems to these "servants" great honour to boast that they are loved or have been loved by a great lady or a woman of good name, how could they keep quiet about it if it was *true*? For God knows how they lie! And may it please God that you ladies may be well aware of this, for you will need to protect yourselves against it.

'Furthermore, do you imagine that the servants who know your secrets and in whom you must put your trust are going to keep quiet about it, even though you have made them swear? Certainly most of them would be very unhappy if it was not known that they had greater intimacy and familiarity with you than the others had. And if they do not tell your secrets with their mouths, they will show them twice as much by means of various subtle signs that they quite intend people to notice. O God, what servitude it is for a lady (and for any other woman in such circumstances) who will not dare to reprimand nor rebuke her servant! Let us suppose that she sees her servants blatantly misbehave while she feels herself to be at their mercy: they will be so arrogant towards her that she will not dare breathe a word, but rather she must suffer them to do and say things that she would not tolerate from anyone else. And what do you think those men and women say who notice this? They think only what is plain to see, and you may be sure that they whisper about it a good deal. If the lady becomes angry or dismisses such servants, God only knows whether all may be revealed and divulged in numerous places. It is often the case that they are and have been go-betweens and panders in this love affair, which they have gladly and diligently sought to arrange in order to gain for themselves gifts or offices or other rewards.

'Most revered lady, let me put it this way: you may be sure that one could as easily plumb an abyss as enumerate all the perils and evils in this kind of amorous adventure, and do not imagine otherwise, for it is exactly as I have said. For these reasons, dearest lady, please do not get yourself involved in such a dangerous predicament. If you have had any thought of it, for God's sake please abandon it before greater evil befalls you, for early is very much better than late, and late better than never. Now you can see what gossip there would be if your new ways continue, when they are already noticed and talk is going around in many places. I do not know what more to say to you, except that with all my heart I humbly beg you not to be angry with me for this, but please understand the good will that prompts me to say it. I should prefer to do my duty and admonish you loyally and perhaps incur your anger than to counsel your destruction or to bring it on in order to have your favour.

'Most revered princess and my dearest lady, I pray God that He may give you a good and long life.'

Part Two

1. This begins the second part of this book, which is addressed to ladies and maidens, and first, to those who live in the court of a princess or a great lady. The first chapter describes how the three ladies, that is, Reason, Rectitude and Justice, recapitulate briefly what has been said before.

After what we have said to queens, princesses and great ladies concerning correct doctrine and teachings pertaining both to the soul and to a good and virtuous character in keeping with the high station and nobility of women who are adorned with honour above all others, we will address our remarks in the second part of this volume to ladies and maidens and ordinary women, both those who dwell at the courts of princesses, having their position conferred upon them by their service, and those who live on their own lands in castles, manors, walled towns and fortified cities.

From the outset we should like to make clear that although it concerns the same doctrine in many points, pertaining to the soul as much as to manners and virtues, and as much to ladies and maidens and all other women as to princesses, we do not intend to relate all over again everything that has been said before, for it would be a needless effort, and it could be tedious for the readers. What is said applies to all women, and each one may take from it whatever she feels she needs for the good and profit of her soul and her character. It is just as necessary for the greatest princesses as for ladies, maidens and other women always to have before their eyes and in their memory the love and fear of Our Lord, who reminds them of the blessings that they receive from Him, that is, the soul that is created in His image, which if they wish to expend a little effort on it will possess forever the Kingdom of Heaven. Now, the understanding necessary to know God and the difference between right and wrong is no small gift, neither is the gift of bodily health and strength to put the good into effect, nor is the abundance of other great blessings. For this reason they are obliged to love Him; one of the very Commandments of the Law, and the first, says, 'Thou shalt love the Lord thy God with all thy heart, and with all thy soul, and with all thy mind', and they ought never to forget it. They should remember fear, too, in thinking of the great punishment of His justice, of which those who do not go by the right path put themselves in peril. This love and fear, if it is rightly in their hearts, will protect them from vices and guide them to the virtues, subdue pride in them and promote humility, drive away wrath and bring patience, repel avarice and extend charity; it will remove envy from them and give them real love towards their neighbours. The love and fear of God will expel idleness and encourage carefulness and diligence in doing good. It will make them hate gluttony and love sobriety; it will banish debauchery and attract chastity. Thus it will promote all the virtues auspicious to the soul and will drive away the vices that can harm it. Moreover, it is just as applicable to ladies, maidens and other women to have worldly prudence in regulating their lives well, each according to her estate, and to love honour and the blessing of a good reputation. So we begin.

2. Four points are described: two good to adopt and the other two to avoid, and how ladies and maidens at court ought to love their mistress. This is the first point.

Once again we three sisters, daughters of God, named Reason, Rectitude and Justice, speak as before. First to you ladies, maidens and women of the court in the service of princesses and great ladies: everything that we have already said can apply to your well-being and the betterment of your characters. But to those good admonitions we will add four points: the first two good to follow and the others to avoid. The first two are not merely good to adopt, but are very necessary to you for the good of your souls and the honour of your persons.

Of these two points, the first is that with all your heart you must love your mistress, that is, the princess in whose service or retinue you are, as you love yourself. The other point is that you must be in your manner, speech and all actions not too familiar nor intimate with men. We will teach you in a moment the reasons that prompt us to say this. As for other good habits that you ought to cultivate, because it has already been said before how the wise princess will maintain you in good order, in simple and good clothing without fripperies but sufficiently rich and well made to be seemly, how you should have a composed manner and be restrained in speech, demeanour and chaste games, we will pass over these points, because anyone who wishes may see them above in Chapter 17 of the first part of this book.

According to our first point of the two we have just mentioned, the lady or maiden of the court (or any servant-woman) is expected to love her lady and mistress with all her heart (whether the mistress is good or bad or kind), or otherwise she damns herself and behaves very badly, and the same is true of all servants as long as they depend on wages, pensions or salaries from anybody. If you ask, 'But truly, if my master or mistress is a bad person or doesn't treat me very well, am I still obliged to love her?'

We answer you, 'Yes, certainly.' For if you think that your employers are bad and that it is not to your advantage to work for them, you must leave them. You should leave if it seems better not to stay there any longer doing your duty badly and not bearing such love to them nor such faith as you owe them. Let us suppose that your employer fails to do her duty: because of that you must not neglect to do yours as long as you are there, or else you should go elsewhere, for you must realize that if you shirk your duty as a servant you damn yourself. It is our intention to describe the extent of this love that the lady or maiden of the court will have for her mistress; love will prompt her to have faith and loyalty in all circumstances.

How can she have faith and loyalty in all circumstances? First of all by loving very greatly the welfare of the lady's soul, in such a way that she will look after her with great care and strongly urge her always to do the right thing, and she will not provide her with the opportunity to do otherwise. As much as possible she will do good deeds without drawing attention to herself. It is a good idea to try not to pass on any gossip to her mistress, whatever it may be, that could tend towards the detriment of her soul. That is, she should neither malign another nor speak against decency and honour, nor should she indulge in wicked talk or stories by which she may disturb her mistress. Furthermore, she will look after her welfare in what is within her duty to do, in avoiding to the best of her ability the company of those who may be given to unseemly excesses. And above all else she will strive to maintain her mistress's honour in deed, in speech and in words, more when she is not present than when she is, and she will increase her good reputation.

She will be very careful, however, as she loves the good of her soul, not to flatter her mistress in order to be more in her good graces, as many servants of all manner of masters and mistresses do, and especially those of great lords and ladies. That kind of thing displeases God greatly and Holy Scripture condemns it in no uncertain terms. To explain more exactly what flattery is so that no one may misunderstand, we will describe the difference between being a good servant and being a flatterer. You must serve well and loyally to the best of your ability and very carefully look after the honour and advantage of all kinds of masters and mistresses; you should devote great care and diligence to pleasing your mistress and serving her in all lawful and honourable things. You must do this quite as much in order to do your duty as to acquire her favour, so that you may be the better for it because it is your bounden duty. If she is ill or unhappy, you must be as sad as if it were your own misfortune, and likewise joyous at her well-being and prosperity. When you see her displeased, be sad with a sorrowful expression, and when good comes to her be joyful, and not just in front of her, but even more when you are out of her presence. Excuse her if you hear evil said, and spread her honour and good name. To do such things with a good heart is not flattery, but rather they are signs of true love and pure loyalty borne by a good servant to a master or mistress.

The out-and-out flatterer behaves like this: if you knew that your mistress (or master) had some vicious inclination to the detriment of her soul, her honour and good character, and if you supported her in this by giving her advice that could uphold and strengthen her in her sin, and you prompted these actions in word and deed, or you heard her say untrue words against the good of another, or support bad or dishonourable opinions, and you said, 'My lady (or my lord), you are quite right!', or if you gave her to understand that she was excellent, good or wise or that it would be good for her to do something that you thought would please her, but it went against the dictates of your conscience – if you did such things and other similar ones that could come up, truly you would be flattering and you would be committing a mortal sin. Besides damning yourself, you would likewise be the cause of your master's or mistress's damnation. God knows all about how many servants of young people and of others behave themselves in such situations! For in order to have their favour and attract their affections there are many who not only support them in wickedness, but they themselves actively seek out and try to find ways of drawing their masters, and even sometimes getting their mistresses, into vile sins and all kinds of vices. Such people are not loyal servants, but rather they are perfidious and wicked. Those who are led into wrongdoing are so blind themselves that they do not notice what is happening. And therefore a doctor of the Church said quite rightly that the flatterer by his talk might as well drive a nail into the eye of his master or mistress; that is, he blinds him or her by his flatteries.

But to get back to our subject, one could here ask this sort of question: 'If a lady or maiden serves a princess, or another lady, whoever she may be, and this mistress should wish to throw herself into an illicit love affair with some man, surely the servant-woman is obliged by the loyalty that she owes her to support her and conceal her actions from everyone else?' It may be that some people would not imagine they were wrong in thinking: 'I must protect the honour of my mistress and conceal her actions, even given that I have not arranged the thing. She wishes to go ahead with it, and if she does not confide in me she could confide in someone else who perhaps would not conceal it so well as I would.' The true answer to this question is that the servant would do evil in whatever case arose, and there is never any excuse for doing evil. Indeed, you cannot support or uphold your mistress in sinning without sinning yourself, nor without being a participant in wickedness. Let us suppose that you say that you do it in order to protect her honour; if you examine your conscience well, you will find that another cause motivates you more, that is, to have more of her favour and to profit in financial terms. But whatever cause prompts you to do it, you do wrong, and in so doing you resemble the blind man who leads another blind man and both stumble into the ditch.

Here is what you will have to do if you wish to practise good sense and have a good conscience. If your mistress trusts you so much in such a case that she tells you her secret, you must reply something like this: 'Madam, I thank you for having such confidence in me that you tell me so much of your very private secret, for if you did not have confidence in me you would not have told me. Never doubt for an instant that your secret is safe, for I promise you loyally that as long as I live it will never get to be known because of me. But truly it grieves me deeply that you have set (or wish to set) your heart on such a thing, for nothing can come of this for you but damnation to your soul and great danger and dishonour to your body. If there is no way in my power to dissuade you from this idea, there is nothing that I can do about it, but (and pardon me for saying it) for my part

I prefer the salvation of my soul and a clear conscience (which would have this on it) to your service, even if you should hate me for it and dismiss me. I would rather have your hatred for doing the right thing than your favour for condoning evil. I would rather die than not try to dissuade you from this plan. I know very well that I am in your service and that I must obey you, but in a situation like this I would be committing a sin, and I am not obliged to do that for anybody on earth.'

The good servant ought to make that sort of reply to her mistress in these circumstances. But if she is sensible she will, however, resist the temptation to go about bragging as many women perhaps do, who, in order to make out that they are very good, tell everyone, 'She begged me to do such-and-such a thing, but I well and truly refused her! I would rather that *she* burned!' And such other things about which it would be better for them to keep silent. So that is the way the good and discreet lady, girl or other woman ought to behave towards her mistress.

However, so that we do not forget to say anything on this subject that may be good, this precept does not mean that if for some reason some calamity occurred, the good servant ought not to protect her mistress in all dangers and defend her as she would her own child. This is just what happened in the case of a lady whose maid prevented her from being surprised in a compromising situation by which she might have lost her honour. As soon as she learned of the situation the maid shrewdly went to the barn and started a fire so that everyone would rush there, and her mistress meanwhile could get away. Another maid found her mistress in despair and wanting to kill herself for shame of being with child without being married. She comforted her and dissuaded her from this wicked wish and let it be known that she herself was pregnant so that when the child came she could say that it was hers. By this means she saved her mistress from death and protected her from dishonour. Since the deed is already done and advice is sought about it, in order to protect another person from despair or from taking the wrong course of action, provided that one is not an accomplice to the act of sin, it is not wrong to do this sort of thing, but a very great charity. Everyone ought to have pity on the sinner, for God does not wish his death, but wishes him to reform and to live; such a one has fallen into sin but afterwards may rise out of it and lead a just life. The servant of the mistress should not be an accomplice either in matters of love or in anything else where there could be sin and vice, for no one is obliged to obey another person if it means disobeying God.

3. This explains the second point that is good for women of the court to observe, which is how they ought to avoid too many friendships with men.

The second point and teaching, as we have said, is that women of the court of whatever rank they may be must guard against having too many friendships with various men. We must give the reasons that move us to say this, for many women could perhaps imagine that it was more suitable and more permissible for them to be familiar with men than other women, but those who think so are deceiving themselves, and we will demonstrate it to you by two principal arguments.

The first is that above all other women, those of the court must preserve their honour (we will explain the other argument in a moment). We say that they must preserve their honour more than other women because their honour or dishonour reflects and rebounds upon their mistress, for if they are well or badly disciplined she will get either the credit or the blame for it. (This has already been mentioned in the first part of this book.) Now the fact is that there is no other lady to whom so much honour is owed as to a princess. It would be to her detriment if there was any blemish in her servants, for people would say, 'Like mistress, like servant.' And so I conclude that they ought to be more careful than others.

To come to our point, there is absolutely no doubt that women, whoever they may be, who delight in being friendly with many men, and even if they do not think that there is anything wrong with it, but rather that it is for laughter and amusement, will scarcely be able to continue these friendships without their being talked about unfavourably, and not only by envious strangers who ceaselessly consider how they can abuse others, but, indeed, even by many of those same men with whom the women are friendly. For women do not suspect that before these men have frequented them for very long some or most of them will try to seduce them if they can. When the men see that many frequent the place where they all would like to be received privately, they wickedly jump to conclusions and invent lies about one another. They make jokes behind the backs of the women, whatever polite manner they may have adopted towards them to their faces and however gracious they appear to be. And this is perfectly true: these jests and comments are reported in towns from mouth to mouth in taverns and other places, everyone adding to the story and putting in his own bit. In this way without cause and without reason as far as committing a sin is concerned, but only because of the simpleness of the women who do not think of the consequences, some are often accused wrongly, even by those to whom they are cordial and who would not believe the allegations if they stopped to think about them. May it please Our Lord that ladies and maidens at court (in truth all women everywhere) may know for certain what such 'friends' say of them. They would have good reason to take back their friendly manner; it would be better for them to have less amusement than so much gossip. Seeing that the men smiled at them before and promised their service and their lives, they would scarcely be able to believe this treachery. 'But,' you might ask us, 'how can this be? Isn't it better, even to protect honour, to be pleasant to everyone than to be friendly with just one or two men? For others may say, "Only so-and-so frequents such-and-such a place; they are in favour but others are not received."'

We answer you that undoubtedly there is nothing to choose between these two evils. It is wrong, that is, against honour, if several frequent the lady (as has been said), and wrong it is if people see only one, two or three frequent her in such a way that they may have suspicions about it. Neither the one way nor the other is good.

'But,' you will say to us, 'in that case will women (especially of the court) be so subjugated that they will not dare to see a soul nor to amuse themselves where gentlemen are present without the bad opinion of society?' I reply that although it is unpleasant, submission is good when it prevents a greater wrong, just as the bridle annoys and displeases the horse, but nevertheless keeps it from stumbling into a ditch. As for their not being pleasant and friendly, where it is suitable in time and place they may enjoy themselves decorously in honourable company; it is not our intention to restrain them in this. We do not say that if at some court or other in France or elsewhere the prince or princess receives strangers, either princes or other excellent knights or squires, it is not most fitting that they be entertained and made welcome among ladies and maidens, for it would be contrary to honour not to do this. We mean only those who by quite bold habit would visit the court without having any other excuse for it than to play and divert themselves in the apartments of the ladies and maidens. What we say ought not to distress anyone, whether she is young and spirited or otherwise, if she loves honour, no more than it ought to displease someone who holds his health dear when the doctor tells him, 'You must use such-and-such a medicine for such-and-such an illness.' That will do for the first reason.

The other reason can concern other honourable women as well as those of the court. It is this: the more a thing is worthy, noble and precious, the more it ought to be valued for its rarity and held in great esteem. And so it is that each honourable, good and wise woman ought to have the reputation for being an excellent treasure and a notable and singular person, worthy of honour and reverence. Since she is like this and wishes to be considered so, it is not appropriate that she be too generous with her greatest treasures, that is, with the intimacy of her most honourable person. The greater the esteem in which she holds herself in regard to all men (not out of pride, but out of a dignity seemly for a woman), the more she will be revered and the more she will turn it to good account. For a thing is never so eagerly seen or desired as when it is good and beautiful and is seen with difficulty. Therefore, we say to respectable women that they must not be too flirtatious and that no good can come of using unchecked language and receiving too many men friends.

4. The third point, which is the first of the two to be avoided: the envy that reigns in court and from what it comes.

Now we will come to the other two above-mentioned points, which are to be avoided principally by women of the court, but also by all women of honour, although they are quite common and prevalent everywhere (especially very abundantly at all courts, more than other places). They are two bad and extremely damnable vices and they attract countless others. The one, and the principal of the two mortal vices, is that most pitiable sin, hated by God – envy. The other is the vice of slander. We will speak of the first one now and afterwards the other.

Since we are disposed towards the good of you all, we would like to apprise you of the remedies that we teach anyone wishing to practise justice and enjoy a good conscience. First of all, in order to understand better the quality or nature of this false envy, we must consider why and from what it originates. It indubitably arises and comes entirely from pride, which engenders it in people who are not on their guard against it, always having before their eyes their poor fragility and their having come from nothing. Rather, they are presumptuous through a foolish arrogance that a proud heart puts into their heads, so that they forget their paltriness and their vices and consider themselves to be worthy of great honours and of great wealth even without having deserved them. Since people are very commonly thus deceived in their own minds, each one tries to outdo his neighbour and to surpass him, not in virtues but in greatness of position, honour or possessions. But when he lacks this grandeur, or he sees someone else more advanced in it than he is or thinks he is, or he is afraid that someone else may achieve a position as high as his own, then he feels full-fledged envy. Although at the court of princes and princesses honours and worldly ranks are distributed more widely than elsewhere, we say (and it is true) that that is the very place where envy principally reigns, because each person who frequents the court would wish to have the greatest part of those goods and honours.

But to get straight to the point, in speaking to any woman of the court of whatever rank she may be, who may be living there because of her rank or to serve the princess, we say that if she wishes to make use of good counsel she will so well govern her heart with wise and good reason that she will never have in herself the fatal worm of this treacherous envy, which destroys the soul of the one who harbours it and gnaws at and kills the heart and the will.

5. *More of this same teaching to women: how they will take care not to have the vice of envy among themselves.*

What will a lady do then to avoid this terrible thorn of envy, and to keep it out of her heart? The wise and good lady, or anyone else living at court, will rise above the incidents that cause an envious heart at the court of a princess. That is, however great a lady may be, if she sees or notices or if it is drawn to her attention that her mistress shows someone else more favour than she does her, or often confides in another person and prefers her to know her secrets and be around her more, she will not suffer because of it, nor will the vice of envy overcome her.

However, in such a case the darts and stings in her heart from this foul envy may lead her to say to herself, 'How is it possible that my lady holds this or that person more in favour than you? How can she want her around her more and let her in on her secrets more? Aren't you of her lineage or more noble than this person is; how can she be better suited to it? Or you are more prudent or a woman of more merit or more cut out to be her confidante. And is it also appropriate that such-and-such a one who has come from nothing or who does not know anything or who is not up to much can promote herself to such an extent or try so hard to be in great favour before the others? Is it right that my lady should advance her so much and make her as welcome as she does or give her such finery and grant her such rank? She is already more advanced in this short time that she has lived here than you who have been here from childhood! How can this be? There is some reason for it, but I will put obstacles in her way if I can and take her down a peg or two! I know quite well how to do it. I know certain things about her. And if I don't know them I will make them up or I will embroider them! She wishes very wickedly to put herself before the others and is already playing the mistress. She wants to get above the others and put them below her. But I will put obstacles in her way if I can, whatever the outcome may be, and whatever the lengths I must go to! I can't stand it any longer! Now she even wants to take *my* place, and my lady tolerates it and encourages her and wishes her to go before the others, but she will not get away with it!'

Such or similar are the goads of envy. But soon by good counsel and a just conscience the wise lady or maiden of the court will reject them. She will be her old self again, saying, 'O foolish dreamer, what can you be thinking of? What do you care about all these treacherous things? What does it matter if you do what you can loyally in all things and you don't have such great rewards for it in this world as somebody else? God, who alone is a just, true judge and who knows all hearts and from whom nothing can be hidden, knows very well what you have done. He will not fail to repay you for it. You should have your hope in Him alone, for the Scriptures say that anyone who has his hope and his faith in princes or in men is damned. If you think that someone else has more wealth and better luck than you in this world, which is only a journey like a pilgrimage, what right do you have to complain or to be mournful about it? Do you want to prevent princes and princesses and powerful persons from treating their underlings as they wish? If your mistress or lady gives her favour to another more than to you, what wrong does she do you? None. Our Lord gave a good example of this in the parable of the workers who were put in the vineyard, of whom some came at sunrise, others at midday and still others in the evening. When he came to make the payment for their day's work, the lord of the vineyard distributed the wages and gave as much to those who had come in the evening as to those who had come at daybreak. The ones who had come first strongly objected. And the lord replied to them, "My friends, what injury have I done you? I am paying you for your day's work exactly what you have been promised. And if I choose to give these workers as much as or more than you, it is no concern of yours. You have no cause to mention it."

'In just the same way you have no cause to complain if your mistress lavishes her favour wherever she chooses when it is none of your business. Furthermore, it may be that you yourself do not know your own faults because you are too lenient with yourself, and your lady knows them well. Your mistress may see another woman who is more prudent, more skilful, and of better breeding and more perfect than you are, and so your lady is more cordial to her, although it may seem to you that you would be the better choice. If you pay close attention to the truth of your conscience and review your actions, you will perhaps find that you may well have deserved it for something that you said or did that was reported to her and angered her, something that you should not have done or said, and she does not love you the better for it. Many others might have dismissed you for it if you are to blame, so you have no cause to be so angry. Perhaps you were too complacent and too proud, and you assumed that nothing could harm you. Now be content with your lot, and do not complain about it except to yourself. Furthermore, do you know what good and what service to God this person may have done who is so much in favour, although it seems to you that she is not worthy of it, for which He wishes to reward her in this way in this world? You have heard how hidden are the ways of God. It is not appropriate for anyone to judge them by something that he sees, however terrible it seems to him. Therefore you ought not to hinder the advancement of anyone else, but think of your own soul and of behaving wisely and always doing your duty well, for God will be sure to recognize it.

'It is good to serve such a master who is all-wise, all-good and all-powerful; any other service is only an obstacle and a hindrance. Take good care not to commit misdeeds against Him, nor contemplate harming another person out of wicked envy in word or deed nor by any other means, for you will damn yourself grievously, even supposing that someone did deserve it, for God does not wish anyone to take vengeance. By as much as you have thought about it, beg forgiveness of Our Lord, and do not concern yourself with who goes before and who goes behind, who may be in favour and who not, for whatever may be done by others, your worth will not be any the less. Moreover, everyone who sees you thus graciously put up with the pride and presumption of someone else without talking about it or showing your irritation will esteem you for it and love you more. On the one hand, you wish to keep your rightful rank among the others without wishing to supplant anyone else, but on the other hand you want to do it graciously. But take great care that you do not offend your conscience with such trivial concerns nor that you cause anyone trouble nor obstruct her, for the sin resulting from it would be laid at your door.'

Such and similar are the remedies that the well-prepared lady of the court can take against the darts and stings of envy. To show how all people ought to flee and shun this grievous sin, a wise man says: 'I do not know why all reasonable creatures do not banish from themselves the sin of envy above all other vices, for if we consider the nature of all the other sins, there is not a single one that does not give any pleasure to the one doing it, such as in vainglory or pride, or the delight in honours; in gluttony, or pleasure in eating; in carnality, or bodily pleasures; and so forth. These pleasures can seduce a person to love them, although they may be forbidden to the soul. But this wicked and hellish sin of envy does not provide pleasure nor give any joy to the person who is most in its clutches, but only sorrowful thought and agitation of heart and mind, a sad and changed face, and pain and torment that pierces and wounds the soul and produces all evils. In short, envy is prone to all wickedness and to all sins. Nor does this wicked and infernal vice render its master any other good or profit. Because the envious cause hatred, another wise man says, 'Please God that the envious man has such large eyes that he can see all the prosperity and the joy that are distributed throughout the world and enjoyed by many people, to the end that he may have cause to be more tormented.'

6. The fourth point, which is the second of the two that are to be avoided. How women of the court ought to be careful to avoid committing slander. What gives rise to slander, its causes and occasions.

We come now to the second point, which is the other vice that the lady, maiden and woman of the court and all others ought to guard against, that is, the sin of slander, because there is no excuse for slander. To elucidate our case better, we will touch on three causes from which slander commonly comes and arises and which are all common at court, individually and sometimes all three together.

The first of the causes is hatred, the second opinion, and the third is sheer envy. These three causes are indeed wicked, but the one that comes from envy is the least excusable. All three are to be avoided, for in no circumstances is slander praiseworthy, but rather it is a most forbidden mortal sin. For this is against two of the Commandments of God: the one that says, 'Do unto others as you would have them do unto you', and the other, 'Love thy neighbour as thyself.' We will discuss these causes and teach ladies the remedies to use in guarding themselves against them.

First we will touch on the first cause, which is hatred. We will formulate four principal reasons to show why one must not slander another out of hatred, regardless of whatever injury one has received. We do not usually hate someone unless the other person has injured us or, rightly or wrongly, we think he has. Then the injured party is most inclined by hatred and spite to slander the one who she thinks has injured her. This is a frequent occurrence at court. A lady or other woman of the court will find out that some people or a certain person is harming her and getting her in bad with her mistress, or the master, or her friends. This other person or faction may be trying to have her dismissed, and perhaps they will succeed in their intention. This lady or maiden stands to lose her service, her livelihood and her position because of it, and perhaps her honour as well because of the things that she is accused of, perhaps without foundation. Even supposing that there was a good reason for these allegations, she will hate the person who has made them. She will doubtless slander her, in private and in public, if the person is not so great that she dares not speak of her, otherwise it will be very difficult to complain about it in the slightest. Her heart will ache greatly, and it is no wonder, in saying evil and villainy of this person, both what she knows to be true and also things she does not know. This cause of slander (that is, hatred for some wrong) could possibly seem just to some people, but undoubtedly it is not, and here is our first reason to demonstrate why.

God wishes you and expressly commands you to love your enemy and render him good for evil. Whoever acts against God's commandment damns himself and therefore gains nothing, and so it would be more to his advantage to hold his tongue. Furthermore, another trouble comes to him because of it, and that is our second reason: that he or she acts against his or her own honour. A person of great intelligence would never slander her enemy because she would know that it could seem to other people that she wanted to avenge herself with words. This is the vengeance of people with little power and faint hearts that few wise people use.

The third reason is that those who hear someone who bears a grudge slandering her adversaries or enemies will not believe her. They will say that she is saying it out of hatred and it ought not to be believed. The fourth reason is that the person who has already harmed her or is able to harm her will be that much more indignant when she hears that she is slandering her. She will be able to increase the injury and do still worse to her. It would be preferable to receive one injury rather than two.

And so in conclusion, the consequences of slander are well expressed by what is written of the man who decided to declare war on heaven and drew a bow against the sky, and the arrows returned on to his own head and wounded him. In just the same way the slander that the person who bears a grudge speaks of his enemy rebounds on to him and wounds his soul and his honour, as is demonstrated by the four reasons above.

7. Of the same: how women of the court ought to be very careful not to speak evil of their mistress.

The second cause that gives rise to slander is a wrong impression formed in something like the following manner: one person will have the idea that another is bad or at fault in something or in everything, or that she does not always behave well in all circumstances, and for this reason and without knowing the truth of the matter (which is perhaps quite otherwise than she thought), on the flimsiest grounds she will misjudge and slander her widely and blatantly with hardly a second thought. Such situations commonly arise everywhere. Doubtless because of opinion and because of not knowing all the facts of the case, those slander most who already have the tendency to slander anyway. There is commonly not a court of a prince and princess without such slanderers, who for such a cause, that is, opinion only, do not spare a soul, not even master or mistress. Therefore, in speaking of this vice, we must mention the great wrong that every person commits who defames and speaks evil of another, and especially of the one who feeds and cares for him, from whom he has his station and his living. Nevertheless, in many courts, if the servants or those men or women who live there see or imagine they see in a master or mistress any little sign of some vice, because of a wrong impression they will immediately exaggerate the case, saying that the thing that they only suspected is actually done.

To speak directly to women (although it can just as well apply to men): there are a considerable number of women of all ranks in the courts of many countries who, if they see their lady or mistress merely speaking quietly to a person once or twice, or showing some sign of intimacy or of friendship, or if they see some laughter or some merriment, made perhaps out of youth or ignorance and in all innocence, they will jump to the wrong conclusion. If this mistress is slightly merry or in her clothing comely and neat (things that come to many people from good breeding, more to some than to others), these slanderers will soon be ready to misjudge her, and not just in this case but in all others as well in which for little reason they will sometimes form a bad impression of their mistress. But this misjudging is the least of their offences, for she is their lady, who gives them food and shelter and good wages from her coffers. Although these people may well curtsy respectfully to her, with one knee touching the ground, and make deep bows and flatter her a great deal, yet they will not keep quiet about gossip, but they will tell each other their impressions, and they will whisper scandal to each other. In a word, they will be just like the bad sheep that is mangy and infects the others. But all of them, you notice, take care that their mistress does not get wind of it. They will be content as long as it is concealed from her alone. They will even agree with and support her, saying that it would be a good idea to do thus and so. They will laugh at her and talk about her behind her back, and they will embroider the story with invented details. A number of servant men and women also do it, but for our purposes the ladies, maidens and women of the court who behave in this way act wrongly to a very serious degree and commit a much greater sin than if they slandered each other or people other than their mistress. There are five principal reasons for this.

The first: the greater a lady she is, the more is her honour or dishonour celebrated throughout the country than that of another ordinary woman. For this reason, she who defames her does worse, because this slander can spread into many regions. The second, because they betray the one to whom they are outwardly pleasant and obedient. Third, they act against their oath, which was to the effect that they would guard her well-being and her honour. Fourth, they render evil for good to those by whom they are maintained and nourished and to whom they owe their position. And fifth, they judge another, which is contrary to the commandment of God, who says, 'Judge not, and ye shall not be judged.'

Let us suppose now that these women of the court know beyond a shadow of a doubt certain secrets about their mistress, as has already been mentioned, and that she is a very wicked and perverse person. They still ought not to defame her, either among themselves or elsewhere, for words can never be said privately enough that they may not be reported, and these women are obliged to guard her honour and cover her shame. If they hear evil spoken of her they must try to tone down the gossip and explain it away. In truth these women who do otherwise do great dishonour to themselves and they should be held in the contempt their inexcusable actions deserve.

You may say to us, 'But I see something I have reason to talk and gossip about, and there is nothing else very interesting about my work.'

We answer you: 'Go away if you do not like it, but if you need to be employed as a servant and cannot go away because you would suffer too great a financial loss, just keep quiet about it and pretend that you do not see the least thing and that you notice nothing, since it is not within your ability to remedy it, nor is it any of your business. Do loyally what you should and do not get involved in anything else. Pray God that He is willing to help your mistress and that He will give her knowledge. If you see evil, and if you hear someone talk about her, play down the gossip if you can, or if not, keep your mouth shut about it, and for this you will be esteemed the more. God knows that many women who talk about their mistresses do it more out of spite because they are not in on the secret, and out of envy that other women know more about it, than for any other motive or gain.'

Now here is what the good lady or maiden or other person of the court will do who wishes to enjoy a good conscience: she will love the well-being and honour of her mistress, and when she sees her honour decline and her mistress in peril of very unpleasant consequences, and if she does not dare speak to her or admonish her, she will go to her mistress's confessor and not to anyone else. She will tell him secretly and in confession what is being said about her, and the peril in which she is putting herself and the evil that could come to her from it. She will beg him for the love of God to teach her and not accuse her.

8. How it is unbecoming for women to defame each other or speak evil.

Furthermore, the women of the court ought likewise never to rebuke or defame one another, as much because of the sin and other reasons already mentioned, as for the fact that whoever would slyly defame another is herself defamed. For assuredly the person who knows that someone is defaming her will also slander that person, and she may even make up stories. Nor is any man or woman so upright that he or she ought to say, 'I am not afraid of anyone. What could anyone say about me? I know I am blameless, therefore I can talk fearlessly about other people.' But it is foolish for those men and women who say that sort of thing to believe it, for there is always something, somewhere, for which one may be reproached. And the Bible supports this when it says, 'There is no man without offence', that is, without sin, and if you do not have one particular vice, you may have another one perhaps worse, or two, or three. If you were to look deeply into your conscience you would find plenty of faults there. For although your sin is a secret from everyone else, it is not hidden from God, and He alone knows the one who is a good pilgrim. Moreover, it is a very great shame that down in the town or elsewhere they may say, 'The ladies and women of the court certainly know how to slander each other! I have heard about such-and-such a lady or maiden such-and-such a thing, and something else about such another.' In this respect the court of a princess ought to be like a well-regulated abbey where the monks have an oath that they will say nothing to outsiders about their secrets or anything that may happen among them. In just the same way ladies and women of the court ought to love and support each other like sisters. They ought not to quarrel with one another in the ladies' apartments, nor betray each other behind their backs like fishwives, for such things are extremely unbecoming at the court of a princess, and they ought not to be allowed.

We have said previously that the third cause of slander is envy, which makes the slander even less excusable. That is, it is the worst and the most wrong and unreasonable kind of slander. If a man full of hatred speaks harshly of the one who has injured him, it is natural for anyone to feel pain from his wound. If God did not forbid vengeance for the above-mentioned reason, it would be an acceptable thing for you in accordance with human law. He who slanders because of an honest opinion may base his opinion on some evidence or clue that seems clear to him, and he will be sincere in what he says. But he who slanders out of envy does it for no other reason than sheer wickedness, which exists and flourishes in his heart, and therefore it is the more damnable for the man or woman who says it and the more perilous to him or her of whom it is said than any other kind of slander. For never was serpent's sting, thrust of sword or other wound so envenomed or so dangerous as is the tongue of an envious person, for it strikes and often kills both itself and another, and sometimes in both soul and body. For if we wish to look into it, good Lord, how many kingdoms, how many countries, and how many good people have been destroyed by mischievous gossip based entirely on envy! We could find a number of examples of this, but I will leave them aside in the interest of brevity. It is true that the slander of an envious person stems entirely from unmitigated wickedness, for how has some good person or someone who has many of the qualities of grace, nature and fortune deserved to be slandered or deserved for someone to try to make him unhappy? If these qualities come easily to him, or if he is happy and fortunate, this slander may not come from anything factual. Therefore, we conclude, as is said above, that it springs from pure wickedness and, therefore, it is the more damnable. We will say no more about this envy (for enough has been said of it before this in the fourth and fifth chapter of this second part). We have also now said quite enough about ladies, maidens and women of the court.

9. *Of baronesses and how to know what is seemly and appropriate for them.*

Now it is time to talk to ladies and maidens who live in castles or in other manor houses on their estates or in walled towns or cities. We must consider what we can say that may be useful to them. Since their status and powers are different, it behoves us to speak differently about certain things, that is, the rank, style, and regulation of their lives. But as for habits and good works towards God, everything applies to them that has been said before, to both princesses and court ladies in short, to cultivate the virtues and shun the vices. There are many powerful ladies who live in various lordships, like baronesses and great landowners, who, however, are not designated princesses. This name 'princess' does not properly apply to any save empresses, queens and duchesses, except the wives of those who, because of their lands, are called princes by the right conferred by the name of the place, as happens in Italy and elsewhere. Although countesses may not be called princesses in all countries, we will consider them to be numbered among the princesses described above, since they follow closely the rank of duchess according to the dignity of the lands.

First we will address these baronesses, of whom there are many in France, Brittany and elsewhere who would surpass in honour and power many existing countesses, although the title of baron may not be so high as that of count. Nevertheless, the power of some barons is very great because of their lands and lordship and the nobility that they have thereby. The wives of these men have very high rank, and as for the discipline of these ladies, it especially behoves them to be in general more prudent and wiser than other women. We must explain how to increase their knowledge so that they may know how to understand everything, for the philosopher says that a person is not wise who does not know a little something about everything. It is also fitting for her to have the spirit of a man. This means that she ought not to be educated entirely indoors, nor in only the great feminine virtues.

Now let us speak of the most important matters. There is no doubt that if he wants to be honoured according to his rank it is the responsibility of every baron to spend the least possible time at his manors and his own estate, for his duties are to bear arms, to attend the court of his prince and to travel. Now, his lady and companion stays behind, and she must take his place. Although there may be enough bailiffs, provosts, administrators and governors, there has to be someone in charge of them all, and therefore it is proper that she should take on this responsibility. She should conduct herself with such skill that she may be feared as well as loved, for the best fear of all is that which comes from love, as has already been mentioned. Her men should be able to rely on her for all kinds of protection in the absence of their lord, in a situation where anyone would offer to do them any harm. Therefore, it is right that she should know about all sorts of things so that in each case she will know what to do. She should be well informed about and apprised of the legal aspects and the local customs, and which things should be phrased carefully if there is need for great tact towards those who would wish to do her wrong or who are somewhat rebellious or uncooperative. She should be kind, humble and charitable towards the good and obedient ones. She ought to work with her husband's counsellors in all her undertakings and listen to the judgement of the wise old men, so that she may not be reproached for anything she does, and no one may say that she wants to do everything her own way.

We have also said that she ought to have the heart of a man, that is, she ought to know how to use weapons and be familiar with everything that pertains to them, so that she may be ready to command her men if the need arises. She should know how to launch an attack or to defend against one, if the situation calls for it. She should take care that her fortresses are well garrisoned. If she is in any doubt about undertaking any course of action, she should sound out her people and find out what they think, rather than do too much on her own initiative. She should consider what manpower she has and can call upon with confidence if the situation warrants it, and for which she will not have to wait in vain nor accept empty promises.

She should devote some thought to how she will be able to provide for the household until her husband comes back, and what financial resources she has and can find in order to do this. She must do her utmost to avoid overburdening her men, for this is the sort of thing that will provoke their enmity. The lady should speak authoritatively and consistently to her people about the deliberations of her council; she should not say one thing today and something else tomorrow. She will give courage to her men-at-arms by her eloquent words and inspire them to be good and loyal and to do well. If her husband is away and has left her in charge with full authority, the wise baroness should adopt these methods of dealing with problems if some other

129

baron or powerful man should wish to challenge her about anything.

In addition, the approach that we have already described above in the chapters on widowed princesses is also expedient for her. These things are also worth while for her to learn for another reason, and that is that she may understand all the workings of the administration after her husband's lifetime. In other words, if she is left a widow she will not be found ignorant of the state of her affairs, even if everyone is trying to take advantage of her and grab her inheritance.

10. How ladies and young women who live on their manors ought to manage their households and estates.

There is another condition of rank and of life than that of baronesses that pertains to ordinary ladies and young women living on or off their lands outside fine cities. Because barons and still more commonly knights and squires and gentlemen travel and go off to the wars, their wives should be wise and sound administrators and manage their affairs well, because most of the time they stay at home without their husbands, who are at court or abroad. They should have all the responsibility of the administration and know how to make use of their revenues and possessions. Every lady of such rank (if she is sensible) ought to know how much her annual income is and how much the revenue from her land is worth. This wise lady ought to persuade her husband if she can by kind words and sensible admonitions to agree to discuss their finances together and try to keep to such a standard of living as their income can provide and not so far above it that at the end of the year they find themselves in debt to their own people or other creditors. There is absolutely no shame in living within your income, however small it may be, but there is shame if creditors are always coming to your door to repossess their goods or if they are obliged to make nuisances of themselves to your men or your tenants or if they have to try by hook or by crook to get their payment.

It is proper for such a lady or young woman to be thoroughly knowledgeable about the laws relating to fiefs, sub-fiefs, quit rents, *champarts*,* taxes for various causes, and all those sorts of things that are within the jurisdiction of the lordship, according to the customs of the region, so that no one can deceive her about them. Since there

* *Champart*: in feudal law, field rent paid in kind to the lord.

are a great many administrators of lands and of noblemen's estates who are quite willing to deceive their masters, she ought to be well versed in all these matters and take care over them. There is nothing dishonourable about making herself familiar with the accounts. She will see them often and wish to know how they are managed in regard to her vassals so that they are not being cheated or incommoded unreasonably, for otherwise it would be a burden on the souls of her and her husband until they made amends for it. Towards poor people a lady should, out of love for God, be more compassionate than strict.

In addition, she will do well to be a very good manager of the estate and to know all about the work on the land and at what time and in which season one ought to perform what operations. She should know which way is the best for the furrows to go according to the lay of the land and according to whether it is in a dry or damp region. She should see that the furrows are straight and well made and of the right depth and sown at exactly the right time with such grains as are best for the land. And likewise she should know all about the work of the vineyard if it is a wine-growing area. She ought to make sure that she has good workmen and overseers in these duties and not take people who change masters every quarter, because that is a bad sign. They should be neither too old, for they will be lazy and weak, nor too young, for they will always be larking about.

She is careful to have them get up early, but she does not depend on anyone for it, if she is a skilful manager of the estate. She herself rises and puts on a *houppelande** and busies herself at her window so that she sees them go outside, for if they are lazy, the laziness will most likely be shown in an unwillingness to go out. She should often take time to visit the fields to see how the men are getting on with the work, for there are a good many workers who will gladly abstain from working the land and give it up for the day if they think no one is keeping an eye on them. Some of them are very accomplished at sleeping in the fields in the shade of a tree while letting their horses or oxen graze in a meadow, and then they say in the evening that they have done a day's work. The wise manager of the estate will be on the look-out for these things. Furthermore, when the wheat is ripe from the month of May, she will not wait for an unrealistically high price, but will harvest her crop, having it cut by strong and industrious fellows. She will pay them in cash or in grain, and when the time comes that they are harvesting the grain, she will

* *Houppelande*: long, loose outer garment.

be careful that they do not leave any wheat behind them or that they do not try any other tricks not mentioned before that such people are apt to get up to. The lady must likewise be attentive to these matters in the other work on the estate.

The lady should get up early in the morning, for in the establishment where the lady usually lies in bed until late it is unlikely that the household will run smoothly. She will busy herself around the house; she will find plenty of orders to give. She will have the animals brought in at the right time, take care how the shepherd looks after them and see that he is in control of them and that he is not cruel, for shepherds sometimes kill them in spite of the mistress or master. She sees that the animals are kept clean, protected from too hot a sun and from the rain and prevented from catching mange. If she is wise she will often go in the evening with one of her women to see how the sheep are being penned up, and thus the shepherd will be more careful that there is nothing for which he may be reproached. She will have him take special care at lambing time and look after the lambs well, for they often die through lack of attention. The lady will rear the young animals carefully and be present at the shearing and ensure that it is done at the right time of year. In areas where there are broad plains and grazing lands, she will keep a large herd of cattle and grow oats for them to eat, selling a little of it. She will keep oxen in the stable, from which she will make a handsome profit when they are fat. If she has woods she will keep a breeding stock of horses there, which is a profitable thing for whoever knows how to break and train them.

In the winter-time, she will reflect that labour is cheap, and therefore she will have her men cut her willow or hazel groves and make vine props to sell in the season. She will set her young lads to cutting wood for heating the manor house, but if the weather is too inclement she will have them thresh in the barn. She will never let them be idle, for there is nothing more wasteful in a manor than an idle staff. Likewise, she will employ her women and her chambermaids to attend to the livestock, to feed the workmen, to weed the courtyards and work in the herb garden, even getting covered in mud. She and her girls and young women will occupy themselves in making clothing. They will select the wool, putting the best quality to one side to make fine garments for her and her husband or to sell if she needs to do so. She uses the coarse wool for little children and for her women and household. She will make heavy table covers from the wool, and from the scraps she will have the linens trimmed that her chambermaids will spin and weave on winter evenings. They will also make many other things that would take too long to list.

In flat, arable country there is a great need to run an estate well, and the one who is most diligent and careful about it, however great she may be, is more than wise and ought to be highly praised for it. This practice of running the household wisely sometimes renders more profit than the entire income from the land. For example, the Countess of Eu, mother of the fine young count who died on the way to Hungary, was very skilled in this. She was a wise estate manager who felt no shame in occupying herself in the perfectly respectable work of household duties, to the extent that the profit that resulted was worth more annually than all the income from her land. The praise of the virtuous woman recounted in the book of Solomon may be aptly applied to such a woman as this.

11. This describes those who are extravagant in their gowns, head-dresses and clothing.

Since we have indicated in the previous chapter that the ladies living out in the country on their manors and inherited lands ought to advise and counsel their husbands about their living expenses (that is, that they should not try to maintain a grander style of living than their income can support), it seems a good idea to warn those women who wish to live wisely and follow our precepts to avoid the superfluous things and excesses that some women adopt. They should especially avoid two things that, although quite common in other places, stem from the great pride that infects many women. As we are now concerned with that subject, and as those vices and faults can present a great danger to their souls and are not good or becoming even to the body, we will mention them. The first item is the very extravagant head-dresses and gowns that some women wear, and the other is the jostling that goes on when they try to get in front of each other at public functions.

As for those gowns, we must explain that the women who take such delight in them are mistaken. It is beyond doubt that in the old days duchesses dared not wear the gowns of queens, nor countesses those of duchesses, nor ordinary ladies those of countesses, nor young women those of older ladies. But nowadays those rules are in disarray and women wear anything, for no one keeps to the rules in gowns or head-dresses. Whether they are men or women, if they can afford whatever degree of grandeur it may be, they have the idea that they must have the best. Just as sheep follow each other, if people see anyone do some extravagant or inappropriate thing in the matter of dress, they immediately follow him and say that they must do what everybody else does. And they are telling the truth: one extravagant person *must* follow another! But if the majority of people were moderate and had good sense, they would not follow each other in doing anything extreme, but rather the one who had begun it would be less respected and would remain alone in his folly.

I do not know what pleasure there can be in this. It is only a lack of sense which so deceives people, for one is not esteemed more for such sartorial pretensions by any means, but less by sensible men and women. There is nothing more ridiculous than a person, regardless of who it may be, dressed with great and excessive pomp, when one knows quite well that he should not really be dressed like that or that he does not have the wherewithal to maintain himself in such garments, but the time has now come when one sees nothing else. If such people end up in poverty and misfortune, no one should feel sorry for them, for many ruin and impoverish themselves through such excesses who would be comfortably off if they lived moderately. A still greater shame to many of them is that some of the debts they run up are often to seamstresses, furriers, clothiers and goldsmiths, with whom they place their orders at the same time, and then they have to pawn one gown in order to pay for another. God only knows whether they finally pay for what they buy on credit and whether in the end the merchandise costs them double.

We say these things for the benefit of those who dress this way hoping thereby to get ahead of their neighbours, for this causes the vast amount of pride that doubtless reigns today more than ever before. No one is satisfied with his social standing, but rather each one wants to look like a king. God sometimes punishes such pride severely, for He cannot tolerate it. Is this not truly a great extravagance that a Parisian tailor reported the other day? He had made a *cotte hardie* for an ordinary lady who lives in the province of Gâtinais. He had used five ells (according to the Paris measure) of wide Brussels cloth in making it. Three quarters of the train touched the ground, and the full sleeves reached to her feet, and God only knows how correspondingly large the head-dress is and how high the points are! It is actually an extremely ugly and unbecoming outfit, as anyone who really looks at it will agree. The golden mean is the most civilized and the most pleasing course.

These remarks are addressed to the ladies of France, for in other countries clothing is usually worn for longer by both men and women. They do not change from one year to the next, as people do here, where clothing keeps getting more and more elaborate. It seems to us the clothing of Italy especially and a few other places is more valuable as far as the cost is concerned, but although they may be of greater showiness and covered with pearls, gold, and precious stones, they do not really cost as much, for they last for a long time and can be handed on to someone else. But such extravagances of cloth, silks and trailing feathers are in vogue, not to mention many others. And likewise their headgear is more beautiful, for there is nothing in the world lovelier on a woman's head than beautiful blond hair. St Paul had the very same view when he said that hair is the glory of women.

12. Here Christine speaks against the pride of some women.

But pride in these clothes I have described follows from another excess that is most disagreeable to those who look at it in the right way. It is the jostling of women trying to get in front of each other in processions at weddings and other gatherings. God knows the envy and the spite that are stirred up because of this! Many women even hesitate to get acquainted with one another and develop friendships together, thinking, 'If I am friendly to that lady who has a grand manner, I would have to rank below her and see her put before me; however, my spirit couldn't tolerate it, therefore I will not associate with her.' And so for this reason are many women so stand-offish with one another that at gatherings they look at each other out of the corner of their eyes, as much as to say, 'That woman over there isn't quite up to my standard', and they know how to do this little trick very well. Even in Paris there are many women like this whose husbands are a bit elevated because they hold some royal office. But what is still worse is what these ladies, maidens and others do in church, a place where more than any other place all sin ought to be avoided. It is more serious when it is committed or thought there than somewhere else, for that is the place of prayer in the service of God the Creator, as He Himself declares in the Gospels. The way they jostle to get in front of each other on the way to the offertory is sinful and impertinent. This custom is practised still more in Picardy and Brittany than in France, for one has often seen some women so presumptuous that they seize each other by the hand right in the church and behave outrageously to one another. The same thing happens when they take the Kiss of Peace.

But what makes it even worse is that the wicked husbands (for there are such) get them started and actively encourage them in this folly. Or alternatively, if they do not do that, they grow angry with their wives, thinking, 'I have a greater claim to nobility than a certain other man, so my wife should take precedence over his.' And the other will think in his turn, 'But I am richer, or hold a higher post (or something like that), so I will not stand for his wife taking precedence over mine!' And so it sometimes happens that for this reason the silly men even get into a fight over it. Good Lord, what presumption and what senselessness! Such outrageous behaviour absolutely ought not to be allowed among Christians! The curates and priests, or even the bishops, who have more power, if the ordinary priests do not dare to, ought to prohibit these goings-on in their jurisdiction, especially in church. For truly it would be better for such women to stay at home than to take such scandalous behaviour there with them. When such pompous people come to the altar, apparently to make an offering to God, but instead making an offering to the prince of Hell, who is the father of Pride, the priests ought to turn their backs and not accept their offerings.

Likewise the Kiss of Peace – they should hang it up on a nail and let whoever wants to kiss it do so.* Undoubtedly, those of whom we speak fervently kiss the object called the 'Peace'; however, they do not make peace but rather war, since their hearts are full of anger arising from great pride. It is certainly a foul and odious habit these women have of envying each other like this during the Kiss of Peace at Mass. It is an obstacle and hindrance to devotion to God, for one person passes it on to another who would feel humiliated to take it. And what do such ceremonies accomplish? Since it signifies the communion of peace (which ought to prevail among Christians), it is for the little people just as much as for the great ones. No one who receives things from God ought to refuse to pass them on to another. The truth is that such customs are to be deplored among Christians.

*The Kiss of Peace, or Pax, was conveyed to the laity at Mass in Christine's day by a Pax Brede (or Osculatorium), a small ivory plate with a handle on the back.

But since merely talking about the disease does not affect it, nor does mentioning the remedy cure it, to reduce the morbid swelling of such habitual pride would be a great act of charity and greatly to the profit of many souls. We have already mentioned before that the bishops might try to remove these ugly customs by excommunicating (after the prohibition) all those, both men and women, who would wish to continue them, and it would be all to the good. As for those who arrogantly wish to raise themselves in such great pomp – certainly great follies lead them to that! For you, Man, if you really want to contemplate the wretchedness of your beginnings, where you are and where you are going to be, you have no reason to be proud of yourself. If you argue that your nobility impels and leads you to desire such honours, let us inform you that no one is noble if he does not have other noble qualities, virtue and good manners. If you do not have these qualities in you, no matter who you are, you are not noble. And if you think you are, you are deceiving yourself.

All the ancient holy doctors of the Church who have mentioned this matter acknowledge this very thing and have written that the greatest is not the one who is full of pride and most elevated in honour and rank, but the one who is most virtuous is the one who is humble. St Augustine, in the book of sayings of Our Lord, speaking especially to you, says, 'Be it known to those who imagine themselves to be noble only because of blood and disregard virtues: you are greatly deceived to think so. You delight in your exalted position and in being considered great. You decide to climb further, but you do not know the path very well, and soon you stray from it. You fancy yourself achieving the heights, but you slip down, because the first rung where you wish to set your foot is Pride, which is a very low and vile ditch. But if you will believe me, I will direct you better to the rung that will take you upwards. The first rung is that of humility, and then the other virtues follow. If you climb by that way you will be very noble, and you will go as high as you wish and without any misfortune being able to harm you.'

After these matters it remains for us to speak of the ladies and maidens who live in fine towns and walled cities, for we hope to say something for the increase of the well-being and honour of everyone. Gentlemen often marry their daughters to rich men living in cities and good towns, of whom some are knights or officers of the king or princes, and others are well-to-do burgesses or wholesale merchants. These girls are not always the worst married, if they wish to accept the situation willingly and are not misled by prejudice. But it sometimes happens that some of them, through a lack of sense and a great deal of pride, are not content, because they regard their husbands as peasants compared to them. This is great foolishness, as is demonstrated above, for no one is a 'peasant' if he does not commit base acts, nor noble if he is not virtuous. Therefore, if they are noble and well-bred women, they ought to show it by good manners and virtuous deeds, for, as the Book of Ecclesiastes says, if you are great and you humble yourself, your greatness and honour will increase by that much more, for by that much will you be more esteemed. As for those well-bred women, the more they humble themselves before their husbands in obedience and in reverence and the faith that marriage requires, the more their honour will increase. For although all women should do this, those women will be esteemed for it still more than the others. And if in groups of other women they are found courteous, humble and kind, and if they are not too overbearing to their households nor too anxious to be waited on hand and foot, and if they are amiable and kindly to everyone, of honourable conduct and actions, and moderate in clothing, they will be a good example to other women. And it will be said of them what is said in the common proverb: 'He who is good, prudent, and wise smells sweet as a rose.'

13. The proper behaviour for ladies in religious orders.

Since we have spoken of the instruction of ladies and young women in various high social positions, the ladies in religious orders who were born for reverence to God, to whom they were given and married, can easily go in this rank – truly, before all others in honour, for reverence for their spouse and religious order, which is, according to God, among the very highest positions. So that our instruction may be generally applicable to all the estates of women, we will speak to them, bearing in mind their way of living, which we say (and it is true) ought to be based on seven principal virtues. We will deal with these virtues according to the sayings of Jesus Christ and the testimony of the holy doctors of the Church. It is to be understood that by the praise of the virtues the vices are condemned, for if it is good to do good, it follows that it is evil to do evil. And as it is a pleasant thing to hear goodness rather than wickedness spoken of, we are pleased out of respect for the holy order to adopt this approach.

So we say to you ladies of religion that, although you are quite familiar with the lessons of your statutes and rules to maintain the institutions established by your founders, we hope it may not be a hardship for you to hear us repeat (if it is agreeable to you) the principal virtues that are essential for you to have. There are seven particular ones, to wit: the first, Obedience, on which is based all order; the second, Humility; the third, Sobriety; the fourth, Patience; the fifth, Solicitude; the sixth, Chastity; the seventh, Concord and Benevolence. Although our words are addressed to those among you in religious orders, it ought to be understood that all women can equally well lend an ear to them and take away whatever they can profitably apply to themselves. And also if any jot or tittle of this can find its way to men, please do not scorn it and throw it to one side, for good precepts can be compared to the good and loyal friend who, when he cannot help, at least does no harm.

Concerning this virtue of Obedience on which religion is based, we cannot praise it more highly than Holy Scripture itself does; saying of Our Lord that He Himself personally demonstrated it to the extent that He was found obedient even unto death. Obedience is to be understood in three principal parts: that is, to obey God in always keeping His Commandments, for nothing else should come before Him; then to obey established laws; and finally to obey one's sovereign. So therefore, the nun ought above all to keep God's Commandments, then to uphold the established law of her order contained in the articles and rules, and thirdly to obey her abbess or prioress. As for the first, everyone knows very well that whoever breaks the Commandments of God commits a mortal sin, but since belonging to a religious order is more worthy and higher than another station of life, a monk or nun sins more mortally than another if he falls into sin. There are several reasons for this, of which one has already been mentioned: that is, because they are in a holier station of life, just as the chamberlain of the king would do worse if he committed some crime against the king's majesty than would a man who did not have the king's faith or confidence or did not hold any royal office. Furthermore, they would be acting against their vows, which bind all those who serve only God with all their power and concentration and who avoid sin at all costs. So you ladies ought to be very careful that you do not transgress any of the articles of , for you would sin grievously; such things would be a sin to you that would not be to secular people, because it would be your institutions you would be disobeying. In addition, the commandments of your sub-prior ought not to be difficult for you, considering the great merit that you acquire in obeying humbly.

The second virtue is Humility, without which, even if you had all the others, you would not be able to please God. As for this virtue being agreeable to God, Holy Scripture shows that the humility of the Blessed Virgin Mary was more pleasing to Our Lord than even her virginity. And that she was agreeable to Him she herself recognizes in her Magnificat, where she says, 'He hath regarded the low estate of his handmaiden.' Indeed, he who would wish to learn about and reap the praises of this virtue of Humility should remember that Holy Scripture says that he must be like the lowest of the low.

The third virtue is Sobriety, which includes Abstinence. To demonstrate that it is appropriate for you, we will refer to the words of St Augustine in the book about the virgin saints where he says that Sobriety is the guard and protection of thoughts, the senses and all the body. It is the custodian of Chastity, and the neighbour of Modesty. It is the companion of Peace and of Friendship and the enemy of all vice. Also Origen says of this very thing that just as Drunkenness is the beginning of all vices, so Sobriety is the mother of all virtues.

Patience is the fourth. But who could recite the great benefits of this virtue? It is exemplified in the life of Our Lord, who is the veritable author of this virtue. Those who are patient may be called the true sons of God, and indeed the Gospel calls them blessed, for the Kingdom of Heaven is rightfully theirs.

The fifth virtue that is essential for a nun is Solicitude or Diligence. Without seeking other proofs, we can show that it is essential for her by referring to St Jerome, who says, regarding the Psalter, that one can overcome nature by virtuous diligence. So that the great benefits may not escape you, you must master even bodily sleep and all your senses, which you can do through Diligence, for even nature can be mastered and controlled by this virtue, that is, by a great desire to attain control over one's own body by the spirit. This is very necessary for a good nun.

The sixth virtue is Chastity, which includes all decency, as much of clothing and head-dress as of words and conduct. If you observe it rightly, this virtue prohibits you from having any garment or head-dress where there is the least worldliness or affectedness, but rather each should be very simple and seemly, according to her order. It is said against some nuns that they wish to look pretty in their tight-fitting clothing, head-dresses and brooches, which is most odious and lewd to see in a nun. Nor is there a more indecent thing to be seen than a nun in an untidy habit. But the mischief is compounded when some wish to dance, frolic about or play sprightly games in mixed company. Certainly they then resemble devils, nor is anything more disgusting nor more abominable than their words if they break the rule of purity and decency. It does not occur to those who adopt such a mode of behaviour that the devil of Hell is in their midst. These are the things that militate against Chastity, and for the love of God, dearest friends, please do not have them in you, for you would be mixing deadly poison with honey for your damnation. Rather, you should delight in this beautiful virtue of Chastity, of which St Ambrose says in the *Book of Virginity*, praising it, 'Chastity makes an angel of man, for whoever practises it is an angel, and whoever loses it is a devil. He who keeps it is a citizen and burgess of heaven.' Of this St Bernard says that just as balm has the property of preserving flesh from decay, so Chastity preserves the soul without corruption and maintains it in cleanliness and confirms it in renown and good odour. For this reason it was said of the good lady Judith, praised by all the nation: 'Thou art the exaltation of Jerusalem; thou art the great glory of Israel; thou art the great rejoicing of our nation, to whom God hath given the strength of a man. Thou hast done much good to Israel because thou hast loved chastity.'

The seventh virtue is Concord, or Benevolence, which is necessary for you and which you ought to love and hold dear in your convents, as the proper place of peace. Hear what St Ambrose in the first book of the *Offices* says: 'Benevolence is like the common mother of all, for it so couples and joins people together that they are brothers, loyally loving each other's welfare and sad at another's misfortune. Removing Benevolence from an assembly of people would amount to taking the Sun away from them.' And then he says, 'Benevolence is like a fountain that refreshes those who are thirsty. Benevolence is a light that lights both itself and others. Benevolence engenders Peace and breaks the sword of Anger. It makes many into one and, to sum up, it is of so great power that it can prevail over nature.' By these things you can understand, dearest ladies, that in true and loyal love you ought to live together like sisters in a union of peace.

And that suffices for the second part of this book.

Here ends the second part.

Part Three

1. How everything that has been said before can apply to one woman as much as to another. Of the system and control that a woman of rank ought to maintain in her household.

At the beginning of this third part, following the description of the path for princesses and then of ladies and young women of the court and outside it, we must now (as we have promised) speak to the women of rank in towns and cities, that is, to those who are married to clerks, counsellors of kings or princes, administrators of justice, or men in various offices. We shall also speak to those who are married to the citizens and merchants of cities and fine towns, who in some countries are called nobles when they are of ancient lineage. Following that, we will address the other classes of women, so that all women may experience our instruction. As we have already mentioned several times before, we intend everything that we have laid down for other ladies and young women concerning both virtues and the management of one's life to apply to every woman of whatever class she may be. It is said as much for one woman as for another, so each one can take whatever part that she sees pertains to her. Please do not do as some foolish people do who are very comfortable when they are listening to a sermon and the preacher is talking about the obligations of some group which does not concern them. They pay close attention to it and note it carefully and say that the preacher is quite right and that it is well said, but when it comes to something that has some bearing on them, they bow their heads and close their ears, and they fancy that they are being badly wronged by being talked about. They are careless about their own actions, but they are keen to hear about those of others! For this reason the wise preacher ought to consider very carefully what kinds of people are listening to his sermon, and if he speaks to some of them, he ought equally to mention the others, so that one group may not be able to scoff at the other nor grumble about them.

We three Virtues therefore repeat what we said before to you women of rank and dwellers in cities and fine towns: please lend an ear to the teachings that pertain to you. There are four principal teachings, although they have been mentioned elsewhere. Your duty to be good and devout towards God goes without saying, but as for what concerns Worldly Prudence: the first of the four pertains to the love and faith that you ought to have for your husbands and how you ought to conduct yourselves towards them. The second point is the matter of the government of your household. The third concerns your grooming and clothing. The fourth is how you may avoid blame and dishonour.

As for the first, which has to do with the love and fidelity that you owe to your spouses and your conduct towards them, whether your husbands be old or young, good or bad, peaceable or quarrelsome, unfaithful or virtuous: so that we need not repeat ourselves, we refer you to the twelfth chapter of the first part of this book, where the matter is set out plainly. But besides this, so that you may find those attitudes more agreeable, we will remind you of three blessings that can come to you from conducting yourselves well and wisely towards them, whoever they are, and keeping your promise to be faithful and loyal to them and holding your peace and in all things doing your duty. The first is the great merit to the soul that you acquire by doing your duties; the second is great honour in the world; and the third is, as one has often seen, that although many rich men of many and varied positions are and have always been remarkably cruel to their wives, when the hour of death comes their conscience pricks them and they consider the goodness of their wives, who have endured them with such a good grace, and the great wrong that they have committed against their wives, and they leave them in possession of their whole fortune.

The second point of our teaching and doctrine that we have said is necessary to you touches on the subject of the household. You ought to devote very great care and diligence to giving wisely, sharing out intelligently and using to the best advantage all the goods and provisions that your husbands by their labour, business or income gather or obtain for the home. It is the duty of the man to acquire all the necessary provisions and to have them brought into the house. Likewise the woman ought to manage and allocate them with good discretion and right priorities without too much parsimoniousness, and equally she ought to guard against foolish generosity, for that is what empties and flattens the purse and impoverishes a person. She should understand that nothing must be wasted, and she should expect all her household to be frugal. She herself must be in overall charge and, always watchful, she must ask for everything to be accounted for.

This wise lady or housewife ought to be very familiar with everything pertaining to the preparation of food so that she may know how best to organize it and give orders to her serving-men or women; in this way she may always be able to keep her husband contented. If he sometimes invites important people to the house, she herself (if need be) ought to go into the kitchen and supervise the serving of the food. She ought to see that her home is kept clean and everything in its place and in order. She should see that her children are well taught and disciplined, even if they are small, and that they are not heard whining or making a lot of noise. They should be kept tidy and established in their own routine. Neither the wet-nurses' swaddling clothes nor anything else that belongs to them should be left lying around the house. She ought to ensure that her husband's garments and other things are kept clean, for the good grooming of the husband is the honour of the wife. She should ensure that he is well served and his peace and quiet are uninterrupted. Before he comes home for dinner everything should be ready and in good order, with tables and sideboards according to their means.

If she wants to act prudently and have the praise of both the world and her husband, she will be cheerful to him all the time, so that if he should be in any way troubled in his thoughts, perhaps by various things that sometimes give rise to problems for a man of property, she may be able by her gracious welcome to get him to put them somewhat out of his mind. It is undoubtedly a great refreshment for a man of substance when he comes into his house with some troubling thought and his wife wisely and graciously welcomes him. It is quite right that she should do this, for the man who is occupied with the burden and care of earning a living can at least be warmly welcomed in his own home. The wife ought not to quarrel with the other members of the household nor nag them nor make a fuss at the table, but if there is something that they have done wrong, she ought to correct them at the time in a few calm words, but at meals, which ought to be taken happily, this kind of thing strikes a very harsh note. If her husband is bad or quarrelsome, she ought to appease him as much as she can by soothing words. She should not ask him about his business affairs or other confidential things at table or in front of the household, but only when they are alone together and in her chamber.

The wise housewife will be careful to rise early in the morning. When she has heard Mass and said her devotions and returned home, she will issue orders to her people for whatever is necessary. Then she will take up some useful work, whether spinning or sewing or something else. When her chambermaids have done their housework, she will want them to do some other work. She will not want to see either girls or women or even herself tolerate any idle hours. She will buy flax cheaply at fairs; she will have it spun in town by poor women (but she will be careful not to take advantage of them deceitfully or by her superior rank, for she would damn herself, and there would be no advantage in it for her). She will have fine wide cloth, tablecloths, napkins and other linen made. She will be most pains-taking about this, for it is the natural pleasure of women and not odious or sluttish, but upright and proper. In the end she will have very fine linen – delicate, generously embroidered and well made. She will keep it white and sweet smelling, neatly folded in a chest; she will be most conscientious about this. She will use it to serve the important people that her husband brings home, by whom she will be greatly esteemed, honoured, and praised.

This wise woman will take great care that no food goes bad around her house, that nothing goes to waste that might help the poor and indigent. If she gives them to the poor, she will ensure that the left-overs are not stale and that the clothes are not moth-eaten. But if she loves the welfare of her soul and the virtue of charity, she will not give her alms only in this way, but with the wine from her own cellar and the meat from her table, to poor women in childbed, to the sick, and often to her poor neighbours. She will do this with pleasure if she is wise and has the means, for these acts are all the laid-up treasure that she will take with her, nor will she ever be the poorer for it. She ought, however, to be careful and have discretion about all her charity.

This woman will be wise and gracious, that is, of pleasant ex-pression, modest, with restrained language; she will welcome and receive the friends and acquaintances of her husband. She will speak nicely to everyone. She will cultivate the friendship of her neighbours; she will offer them companionship and friendship if they need it and she will not refuse to lend little things. To her household staff she will be neither mean, sharp-tongued, nor spiteful, nor will she nag them all day about trifles, but reprimand them properly when they do something wrong and threaten to dismiss them if they do not mend their ways. But she will do this without raging or making a noisy fuss that can be heard in the next street, as some foolish women do who imagine that by being quite disagreeable and quarrelling vehemently about nothing with their husbands and their household servants, and making a lot of work out of only a small job, and finding things everywhere to complain about, and always gossiping, they will be regarded as good and wise housewives. But that kind of housewifery has nothing to do with our teaching, for we want our adherents to be wise in all their actions. There can be no sensible behaviour without moderation, which does not require malice or anger or shouting – all things that are most unseemly in a woman.

2. This describes how women of rank ought to be conservative in their clothing, and how they can protect themselves against those who try to deceive them.

The third point that we want to tell you about – you towndwellers and women of rank in fine towns – concerning your garments and clothing, is that in these you must not be extravagant, either in the cost or in the fashions. There are five particular reasons that ought to persuade you to guard against extravagance. The first: that it is a sin and it displeases God to be so attentive to one's own body; the second: that by making an extravagant show one is not the more esteemed for it, but less, as has already been said elsewhere; the third: that it is a waste of money, an impoverishment and emptying of the purse; the fourth: that you give a bad example to others. (That is, you give them reason to do likewise or worse, for it will seem to a lady who sees a young woman or a townswoman assume a grand style of dressing that by as much as she is greater so should her clothes be finer. This is what makes the pomp and luxurious clothing multiply and increase every day, because each person is always trying to outdo the other – by which many people are ruined in France and elsewhere.) The fifth: that by an inappropriate or extravagant outfit you give another woman the occasion of sinning, either in envious whispering or in a desire to dress above her station, which is a thing that displeases God very much. And so, dear ladies, as this can do you no good and a great deal of harm, please do not take too much enjoyment in such base behaviour. However, it is quite right that each woman wear such clothing as indicates her husband's and her rank, rather than if she is a middle-class townswoman and she dresses like a young noblewoman and the young noblewoman like a lady – and so on, step by step on up the scale. It is indubitably a thing contrary to good public order, in which, in any country, if it is well regulated everything ought to be within limits.

Now we come to the fourth point, which is how you will keep from rebuke and from getting a bad name, to which point the matter of your clothing may be relevant, both in the extravagance or too high a cost and in the sort of fashions. In this connection let us suppose, for example, that a woman is of excellent character and without any bad deed or thought in her head: but no one will believe it, for she is seen wearing clothing above her station. Many bad judgements will be made against her, however good she may really be. It therefore behoves any woman who wants to preserve her good reputation to be modest and conservative in her clothing. Her garments should not be too tight nor the neckline too low, nor should she take up other unchaste fashions, nor new-fangled things, especially indecent ones. Also a lady's manner and expression count for a good deal. For as has already been mentioned before, there is nothing more unseemly in a woman than a disagreeable manner and a sour expression, also nothing more pleasant than a fair countenance and a quiet demeanour. Even if she is young, she ought to be moderate and not disorderly in her games and laughter. She ought to know how to enjoy them in moderation so that they are seemly, and her speech should be without flirtatiousness, but proper and mild, orderly and comely, with a simple and decorous look, and not glancing about; she should be merry, but in moderation.

But to return to the matter that we mentioned above: that is, that besides the talk and blame that can spring up around a woman because of inappropriate clothing and a vulgar manner, there is one other drawback that is more dangerous, and that is the wrong impression given to foolish men who may think that she is doing it in order to be desired and lusted after in illicit love. She will perhaps not think of it at all, doing it only for her own pleasure and because her temperament inclines her to it. There are men of many classes who will try diligently to seduce her, pursuing her with various meaningful signs, and they will exert themselves considerably to this end. But what should the wise young woman do who does not wish to slip into error and who is well aware that nothing can come of such a love affair but all sorts of bad things, harm and dishonour, which these reckless men choose to ignore? She does not want to do as some thoughtless women do, whom it pleases very much to be pursued with great ardour. They fancy it is a fine thing to say, 'I am greatly loved by several men! It is a sign that I am beautiful and that there is much good in me. I will not fall in love with any of them, however, but I will be pleasant to all of them, to one as much as to another, and I will talk to them all.'

This is not the way to protect your honour, but rather it is impossible that this position can long be maintained by a woman, whoever she may be, without her sliding into error. For this reason as soon as the wise lady notices by any sign or indication that some man has designs on her, by her own words and gestures and manner she ought to give him every opportunity to give up the idea, and finally make him realize that she is not interested and does not want to be. And if he speaks to her, she should reply to him along these lines: 'Sir, if you have been thinking about me, please stop it! For I promise you and swear by my faith that I have no intention of embarking on such a love affair, nor will I ever have. I can easily swear this, for I am so strongly confirmed in this conviction that there is neither a man nor any other thing that can dissuade me from it, and all my life I shall remain firm on this point. You may be certain of that! So your trouble is all for nothing as long as you waste your time on this. I beg of you most strenuously not to make any more such overtures to me nor to say these words, for in good faith I will take great displeasure in them, and I will do everything in my power to avoid going where you are. I tell you once and for all, you can be absolutely certain that you will never find me in any other opinion, and so I bid you farewell.'

In this way, briefly and without listening to him for very long, the good and wise young woman who loves her honour ought to reply to any man who importunes her. Moreover, signs and gestures with the same import as the words may be used. In other words, she should not make by either look or demeanour any sign by which he can have a glimmer of hope that he can ever succeed in his scheme. If he sends her gifts of whatever kind, she must take care not to accept any of them, for whoever accepts a gift seriously compromises herself. If any person should give her some message from him, she should say emphatically and with a frown never again to speak of him to her. And if her chambermaid or servant-boy dares to mention it again she will not keep that person in her house, for such servants are not reliable. She will find some tactful way to dismiss the servant for some other reason, without quarrel and without bad feelings.

But whatever happens, she must take great care that she does not mention it to her husband. With the best intentions she might accidentally put him into such a frenzy that she could not pacify him. It is a very great danger but also a needless one, if she takes wise precautions and keeps quiet about it. No man is so determined that he will not give up if the lady really wants him to go away and shows it by her manner. Neither should she mention it to a neighbour, man or woman, nor to anyone else, for words are reported, and men sometimes make up wicked stories about women out of spite at being refused and at knowing that the women are talking or have been talking about them. So it is no hardship to keep quiet about the thing when mentioning it would accomplish nothing. Boasting is not a pretty thing in a woman. Furthermore, women who wish to protect themselves from blame ought to avoid associating with people who are not good and respectable, nor should they attend gatherings made in gardens or in other places by prelates or lords or other people on the pretext of entertaining a group of people, when it may be for a scheme for some assignation, whether for the ladies themselves or for someone else. Let us suppose that a woman knows very well that such a gathering is not meant for her; nevertheless she ought to be very careful not to provide a means of dalliance for others, for it would be the cause of evil and of sin. She ought not to go there if she knows of such a plot or has any suspicion of it; it would be preferable that she not go out at all, anywhere. If she is wise, she ought to consider carefully how and where she goes.

Neither should she use pilgrimages as an excuse to get away from the town in order to go somewhere to play about or kick up her heels in some merry company. This is merely sin and wickedness in whoever does it, for it is offensive to God and a sad shame. 'Pilgrimages' like that are not worthy of the name. Nor should she go gadding around the town with young women, on Monday to St Audrey, on Thursday I don't know where, on Friday to St Catherine, and so forth on other days. Although some do it, there is no great need for it – not that we wish to prevent their doing good, but undeniably, considering the dangers and the thoughtlessness of youth and the great desire men commonly have to seduce women and the baseless talk that is soon circulating about it, the very safest course for the profit of the soul and the honour of the body is not to be in the habit of gadding all over town. For God is everywhere, who answers the prayers of devout supplicants, whoever they may be, and who wishes all things to be done discreetly and not wilfully. Also the warm baths and the gossip sessions and other get-togethers that women frequent too much without need or good cause are only a waste of money, and no good can come of them. Therefore a woman who loves honour, if she is wise and wishes to avoid reproach, ought to guard against all such things and other similar ones.

3. Of the wives of merchants.

Now we come to merchants, that is, the wives of men who deal with merchandise, who in Paris and elsewhere are very rich and whose wives dress expensively and with great show, and even more so in some regions and cities than in Paris, as, for example, in Venice, Genoa, Florence, Lucca, Avignon and elsewhere. But these places (although any place has its excesses) can be excused more easily than these parts of France, because there are not so many distinctions of high rank as in Paris and that area, that is, queens and duchesses, countesses and other ladies and young ladies, by which the ranks are more differentiated. And for that reason in France, which is the noblest realm in the world and where all things ought to be in the best order (according to the ancient usages of France), it is not fitting for women to do what they do in other places (as has been mentioned several times): that the wife of a country labourer enjoy the same rank as the wife of an honest artisan in Paris, nor the wife of a common artisan as a merchant's wife, nor a merchant's wife as an unmarried lady, nor the unmarried lady as a married lady, nor the lady as a countess or duchess, nor the countess as the queen. Rather, each woman ought to keep to her own station in life, and just as there is a difference in the way of life of people, so there ought to be a difference in their estates. But these rules are not kept nowadays, nor many other good ones that always used to be, and for this reason a woman loses the effect that she seeks. For beyond a doubt neither the pride nor the pomp were ever so extreme in all sorts of people from the great to the indigent as they are now; one can see this by reading the chronicles and ancient histories. For this reason we have said that although it is true that in Italy the women still wear greater finery, they do not go to such great expense as they do here, considering the retinues and all sorts of luxuries that ladies go in for. In these things as well as in their gowns they all try to outdo each other.

But now let us say something about merchants' wives. Was this not truly a great extravagance for a wife of a grocer? Even as a merchant, the husband is not like those of Venice or Genoa who go abroad and have their agents in every country, buy in large quantities and have a big turnover, and then they send their merchandise to every land in great bundles and thus earn enormous wealth. Such ones as these are called 'noble merchants'. But this one we are describing now buys in large quantities and sells in small amounts for perhaps only a few pennies, more or less, although his wife is rich and dresses like a great lady. Not long ago she had a lying-in before the birth of her child. Now, before one entered her chamber, one passed through two other very fine chambers, in each of which there was a large bed well and richly hung with curtains. In the second one there was a large dresser covered like an altar and laden with silver vessels. And then from that chamber one entered the chamber of the woman in childbed, a large and well-appointed room hung from floor to ceiling with tapestries made with her device worked very richly in fine Cyprus gold.

In this chamber was a large, highly ornamented dresser covered with golden dishes. The bed was large and handsome and hung with exquisite curtains. On the floor around the bed the carpets on which one walked were all worked with gold, and the large ornamented hangings, which extended more than a hand span below the bed-spread, were of such fine linen of Rheims that they were worth three hundred francs. On top of this bedspread of tissue of gold was another large covering of linen as fine as silk, all of one piece and without a seam (made by a method only recently invented) and very expensive; it was said to be worth two hundred francs and more. It was so wide and long that it covered all sides of this large, elaborate bed and extended beyond the edge of the bedspread, which trailed on the floor on all sides. In this bed lay the woman who was going to give birth, dressed in crimson silk cloth and propped up on big pillows of the same silk with big pearl buttons, adorned like a young lady. And God knows what money was wasted on amusements, bathing and various social gatherings, according to the customs in Paris for women in childbed (some more than others), at this lying-in! Although there are many examples of great prodigality, this extravagance exceeds all the others, and so is worth putting in a book! This thing was even reported in the queen's chamber! Some people will remark that the people of Paris have too much blood, and that the abundance of it sometimes brings on certain illnesses. In other words, a great abundance of riches can easily lead them astray. It would be better for them if the king imposed some *aide*,* impost or tax on them to prevent their wives from going about comparing themselves with the queen of France, who scarcely looks any grander.

Now, such a circumstance is not in the right order of things and comes from presumption and not from good sense, for those men and women who do these things acquire from them not esteem but contempt. Although they adopt the style of great ladies or princesses, they are not really such, nor are they called that, but rather they retain the name of merchants or wives of merchants, even those who in Lombardy would be called not merchants but retailers because they sell in small quantities. It is very great folly to dress up in clothes more suitable for someone else when everyone knows very well to whom they rightfully belong; in other words, to take up the grander style that belongs to another and not to oneself. Even if those men and women who indulge in such excesses, whether in clothing or grand style, left their business and took up the fine horses and the status of princes and lords, their real social position would still dog them. It is very stupid not to be ashamed to sell their merchandise and conduct their business, but yet to be ashamed to wear the corresponding clothing. Truly the clothing is very handsome, fine and respectable for whoever has the right to wear it, and the rank of merchant is fine and honourable in France and in any other country. Such people can be called 'disguised people', and we do not say this to diminish their honour, for we have just said that the rank of a merchant is fine and good for those who deserve it. We say this with the best intentions, in order to give counsel and advice to women. We want to protect them from such unnecessary and wasteful things, which are good neither for body nor soul and can be the cause of their husbands' being assessed for some new tax. So it is to their advantage and it is their best course of action to wear their rightful clothing, each woman according to her own position. Assuming that the women are rich, they may wear handsome, fine and modest clothing without adopting others.

Good Lord, what can such people do with their wealth? Certainly if they stored up treasure in Heaven according to the counsel of the Gospels, they would be well advised, for as we have said before, this life is very brief and the next one is everlasting. It would be a good investment for them for the time to come if they shared their great riches among the poor in true charity. If many did this (and it is

* *Aide*, a feudal tax.

certainly very needful), through this good and noble virtue of charity, which God considers very desirable, they could buy the field mentioned in the parable in the Gospel where the great treasure is hidden. This treasure is the joy of Paradise. Pope Leo speaks nobly of this holy virtue in his sermon on the Apparition, where he says, 'So great is the virtue of charitable mercy that without it the other virtues cannot thrive, for however much any person may be abstinent and devout, guard himself against sin, and possess all other virtues, without this one which gives value to the others it is all for nothing. On the day of the Last Judgement it will be carrying the banner before all the other virtues for those who in this world have loved it and lived by it. It will conduct them to Paradise, and Our Lord will destroy and give his final sentence to those in whom charity is lacking. The text of the Gospels assures us of this.'

If you rich women want to be saved in this way, see that in your business dealings you do not deal fraudulently or deceitfully with your neighbours.

4. Of young and elderly widows.

To make our work more entirely to the profit of all conditions of women, we will speak to the widowed commoners, although we have mentioned this condition above in regard to princesses.

Dear friends, you move us to pity for your fall into the state of widowhood by the death that deprives you of your husbands, whoever they were. This pitiful state usually involves much anguish and much troublesome business. But it happens in different ways – to those women who are rich in one way and to those who are not at all rich in another. Rich women often have trouble because people try to relieve them of their wealth. Trouble comes to the poor or to those who are not rich, because in their affairs they do not find pity from anyone. Besides the grief that you feel at having lost your spouses, which should be enough to have to suffer, there are three principal evils that you should know about very generally, whether you are rich or poor.

The first, which has already been mentioned, is that you commonly find hard-heartedness and little esteem or pity in anyone. Such people as were in the habit of honouring you while your husbands were alive (who were officials or of some high position) are no longer very friendly and have little regard for you. The second evil that afflicts you is the various suits and many requests to do with debts or disputes over land or pensions. The third is the abusive language of people who in the nature of things are inclined to attack you, so that you can hardly do anything without people finding something to criticize. You therefore need to be armed with good sense against these plagues and all the others that can come to you. We would also like to acquaint you with what can be valuable to you, however much we have perhaps spoken of it elsewhere, for as it is pertinent to the present matter, we will remind you of it again.

As for the hard-heartedness that you commonly find in everyone (which is the first of the above-mentioned evils), there are three remedies for it. First of all turn to God, who so wished to suffer for humankind, and if you contemplate this, it will teach you to be patient, which is a quality you will have great need for. The contemplation of God will also protect you in these circumstances if you put your heart into it, for you little realize the ways of the world, and you are about to learn how changeable are the things of this world.

The second remedy is that you must dispose your heart to be kind and gentle in speech and defer to everyone, so that in this way you may conquer and soften the hearts of evil-doers by gentle petitions and humble requests. The third remedy is to be kind and humble in speech, clothing and countenance and consider how with prudence and wise conduct you may defend and guard yourself against those who are bent on tormenting, injuring and oppressing you; in other words, strenuously avoid their company and try not to have anything to do with them. Try to keep close to your hearth and home and not engage in arguments or quarrels with a neighbour, neither man nor woman, nor even with a servant nor chambermaid. Speak softly, but always protect your rights, and by doing this and by not associating much with certain people if you do not need to, you will avoid being injured and dominated by other people.

As for those who bring lawsuits against you (which is the second evil), you ought to know that you must avoid suits and legal proceedings if you possibly can, for it is something that can greatly trouble a widowed woman for several reasons. The first is that she does not know all the ins and outs and is naive in such matters. Secondly, it necessitates her putting herself at the mercy of others in order to have her needs attended to, and people are commonly careless about women's affairs and cheat them when they see the chance and put them to so much expense that they spend eight sous to get six. Another reason to settle the case amicably is that she cannot go to court at all hours* as a man would, and for this reason the best advice is to drop the case even if she loses a little by it, as long as it is not too much. She ought to make every reasonable offer to settle out of court, considering carefully what is asked of her. If she has to be a plaintiff, she should pursue her rights courteously and see whether she can get them by some other means. If she is hounded by debts, she should look at what reason and justification her creditors have. Even if there are no letters or witnesses, if her conscience feels that something is owed, she must take good care that she does not keep what rightfully belongs to someone else, for she would be weighing down both her husband's soul and her own, and God might well send her so many corresponding losses in another quarter that in the end she would lose twice as much. But if she wisely knows how to protect herself against the charlatans who make groundless demands, she does the right thing.

But if eventually she is obliged to go to law, she ought to know that three principal things are necessary to a person who brings a suit. The first is to work through the counsel of wise lawyers and clerks who are very knowledgeable in the discipline of justice and the law. The second is to have great care and diligence in pursuing the case. And the third is to have enough money to do this, for without a doubt, if one of these three things is lacking (whatever good case the person may have), she will be in danger of losing it. So it is necessary for the sensible widow in these circumstances to go to the oldest and most experienced lawyers, the ones most used to pleading different cases (and not the younger ones), and explain her case to them and show them her letters and documents. She should attend carefully to what they say, and not conceal from them anything that can have any bearing on the case, whether in her favour or against it, for they cannot advise her except according to what she tells them. Then she should bring her suit or settle amicably according to their considered opinion. Now, if she undertakes her suit with diligence and pays well for it, her chances will be better. It will behove her to do these things, and likewise resist all her other enemies. If she wants to win, she must adopt a man's heart (in other words, constant, strong and wise) to consider and to pursue the best course of action. She must not collapse like a simple woman into tears and sobs without putting up a fight, like a poor dog who cowers in a corner while all the others attack it. For if you women did this, you would find plenty of pitiless people who would take the

* In Christine's day law court sessions in Paris began between six and seven a.m. in the winter.

bread out of your hand and would consider you ignorant and simple, nor would you ever find any pity in their souls. So therefore, you must not try to go it alone nor trust only in your own intelligence, but get sound advice about everything, especially for important things that you do not know much about.

You widows ought to conduct your affairs in this way, that is, those of you who are older and who do not wish to marry again, but as for young widows, it is seemly that they be governed by their parents and friends until they remarry. They should behave kindly and simply towards those parents and friends, and in such a manner that a bad reputation cannot get started about them, for that would destroy all their advantages.

The third remedy for the three above-mentioned evils to widowed women, who are at the mercy of abusive language, is that they ought to be sure in all respects not to give occasion for defamation or slander about them in any way, whether in their expressions, conduct or clothing, which ought to be simple, modest and decent, demure and subdued. Unless they are relatives, they must not be too friendly nor intimate with any men who are seen to come and go at their houses, even though it is done discreetly. She should be careful with even priests and monks, however devout she may be, because the world is much inclined to say or think evil. Widows must avoid having a household where anyone might have any cause for suspicion; they must not indulge in intimacy or familiarity, however good they know their servants to be. Nor, although the ladies may not see anything wrong with it, should they spend money so lavishly that people talk about it. The better to conserve what she has, a widow should not live in too grand a style, in regard to servants or cloaks or food, for the proper way of life for a widowed woman is to be sober and to do without unnecessary knick-knacks. Since there is so much hardship for women in the state of widowhood (we say it, and it is true), it could seem to some people that therefore it would be better for them all if they remarried. This assumption could be countered by saying that if in married life everything were all repose and peace, truly it would be sensible for a woman to enter it again, but because one sees quite the contrary, any woman ought to be very wary of remarriage, although for young women it may be a necessity or anyway very convenient. But for those who have already passed their youth and who are well enough off and are not constrained by poverty, it is sheer folly, although some women who wish to remarry say that it is no life for a woman on her own. So few widows trust in their own intelligence that they excuse themselves by saying that they would not know how to look after themselves. But the height of folly is an old woman taking a young man! After a while she is singing a different song! It is difficult to feel very sorry for her, because she has brought her misfortune on herself.

5. Of the instruction for both girls and older women in the state of virginity.

In the course of our lessons it would not be right to forget the women or girls who are virgins. They may be in one of two different situations: namely, those who intend to keep their virginity for life for the love of Our Lord, and those who are awaiting the time of their marriage, to be decided by their parents. Just as there is a difference in their intention, there should likewise be a difference in their clothing, circle of friends and way of life, for to those women who have firmly decided never to lose their virginity belongs a most devout and solitary life, and although it may be a seemly sort of life for all women, nevertheless for these women it is even more suitable than for others. If it is necessary for them to do any work to make a living or to be a servant anywhere, they ought to see to it that all their other work comes after they have done their necessary labour of devout prayers in the service of God. This work for God also includes fasts and abstinences, but done using some discretion; they should not be so strict that the women cannot bear them or continue them, nor so harsh that their brains can be addled by it, for nothing of too great stringency ought to be undertaken without good advice. They ought to keep themselves from all sin, especially in deed and in thought, so that the good that they do in one place they do not cancel out in another, for it does little good to be a virgin, or chaste, and make fasts and devotions, and then be a great sinner. Any person who sets out to do good ought to ensure that she offers God a pure offering, for whoever would present the King with an excellent and beautiful dish all mixed up with filth and garbage would not please the King in the least; he would be quite right to refuse it. So their speech must be good, simple, devout and not too garrulous, their clothing chaste and without any fripperies, their behaviour simple and courteous. They should display an expression of humility with the eyes lowered, and their speech should be kindly. It ought to be their joy to hear the Word of God and to go often to church. Those women who have chosen this life are fortunate, for they have taken the best course.

The other virgins who are waiting for the state of marriage ought to be in their countenances, conduct and speech moderate and chaste, and, especially in church, quiet, looking at their books or with their eyes lowered. In the street and in public they should be mild and sedate, and at home not idle but always busy with some housework. Their clothing should be well made, tasteful, tidy and clean, with no indecency. Their hair should be tidy and not dirty or straggling. Their speech should be amiable and courteous to all people; they should have a humble manner and not be too talkative. If they are at celebrations, dances or assemblies, they should be sure to have a gracious manner and excellent conduct, because more people have their eyes on them there. They should dance demurely and sing softly and not stare vacantly here and there. They should not join the men too much, but always seek the company of their mothers or the other women. These maidens ought to take care not to get into arguments or disputes with anyone, neither serving-man nor chambermaid. It is a very ugly thing in a girl to be argumentative and to answer back, and she could lose her good name because of it, thanks to the false and lying reports that household servants often make. A maiden must not be in any way forward, outspoken or loose, especially in the presence of men, whoever they may be, neither clerks in the household service, nor serving-men, nor other members of the household staff. She must not allow a man to touch her on whatever pretext, nor to touch her with his hands in a playful manner, nor to joke with her too much, for that would be very harmful to the respectability and good reputation that she ought to have.

A young girl should also especially venerate Our Lady, St Catherine, and all virgins, and if she can read, eagerly read their biographies. She should fast on certain days and above all be moderate in drinking and eating. She should be content with a small amount of food and with weak wines, for gluttony of wine and food in a girl is above all else an odious blemish. For this reason she ought to take good care that no one should ever see her affected by having drunk too much wine, for if she had such a fault, nothing good would be said of it. So all young girls ought to be in the habit of putting generous amounts of water in their wine, and they should habitually drink very little. Also besides the good qualities and manners appropriate to her, any young girl ought to be very humble and obedient to her mother and father. She should serve them diligently as well as she can, and rely on them to arrange her marriage. She should not make the match herself without their consent, nor should she say anything about it herself nor listen to anyone else talk about it. Young girls taught and brought up in this way are much sought after by men looking for wives.

6. How elderly ladies ought to conduct themselves towards young ones, and the qualities that they ought to have.

There is quite often argument and discord, as much in outlook as in conversation, between old people and young ones, to the point that they can hardly stand each other, as though they were members of two different species. The difference in age ensures a difference in their attitudes and social positions. We should like to make peace in this war between women of different ages. If they can hear our teaching, we will remind them of some things that may be good for them. We will speak first to the elderly ladies of the behaviour proper to them.

It is seemly for any older woman to be sensible in her actions, her clothing, facial expression and speech. She ought to be sensible in her actions because she ought to remember the things that she has seen happen in her lifetime; before she undertakes to do anything she ought to be guided by her experience. For if she has seen evil or good happen to anyone because of having certain habits of conduct, she may think that the same thing will happen to her if she does likewise. For this reason it is said that old people are usually wiser than the young, and it is true for two reasons.

First, because their understanding is more perfect and is to be taken more seriously; second, because they have greater experience of past events because they have seen more. So therefore, they are likely to be wiser, and if they are not, they are the more reprehensible. Inevitably nothing is more ridiculous than old people who lack good judgement or who are foolish or commit the follies that youth prompts in the young (and which are reprehensible even in them). For this reason the elderly woman ought to see to it that she does nothing that looks foolish. It is not seemly for her to dance, frolic about or to laugh uproariously. But if she is of a happy disposition, she ought always to see that she takes her pleasure sedately and not in the manner of young people, but in a more dignified way. She should say her words calmly and indulge in her amusements with decorum and without any rowdiness. Although we say that she ought to be wise and dignified, we do not mean, however, that she should be snappish, bad-tempered, fault-finding or rude, hoping to make people think that those are all signs of wisdom. She ought rather to guard herself against such passions as generally come to old people, namely being wrathful, spiteful and surly. For this reason, when she feels in an argumentative or angry mood, the wise elderly lady will temper it by means of this prudent discretion, saying to herself, 'Goodness, what's the matter with you? What are you trying to do? Is this the behaviour of a sensible woman, to be upset like this? If you think these things are wrong, it is not up to you to put everything right. Calm down and do not speak so spitefully. If you could see how mean your expression looks when you are in such a fury, you would be horrified. Be more approachable and more easy-going to your people, and if you have to chastise them, reprimand them more courteously. Avoid such anger, for it displeases God, and does you no good and will not make people love you. You must be patient.' Such things and similar ones the wise lady ought to say to herself when she feels moved to anger.

Besides having this sensible attitude, the elderly woman ought to be dressed in well-cut and respectable garments, for there is a true saying: an overdressed old woman makes a laughing-stock of herself. Her face should have a fine and honourable expression, for truly, although some may say that it is fine clothing that denotes great honour and respect, this expression is characteristic of an elderly person who is wise and has an honourable manner in all things. The speech of this wise elderly woman ought to be entirely controlled by discretion. She must be careful that foolish, vulgar words do not issue from her mouth, for foolish and crude language in old people is extremely ridiculous.

But to return to what we were saying earlier, namely the disputes and disagreements that generally exist between old and young people: the wise woman ought to reflect on this matter so that when she feels like criticizing young people because of some intolerable fault of their youth, she should say to herself, 'My Lord, but you were young once; cast your mind back to the things you got up to in those days! Would you have liked people to talk about you this way? And why are you so exercised about their affairs anyway? Consider the great trials of youth. You should take pity on them, for you have passed that way yourself.

'One ought to correct young people and reprove them firmly for their follies, but not however hate or defame them, for they are not aware of what they are doing. For this reason you will put up with them tolerantly and gently rebuke them when you have to. And if others criticize or defame them, you will excuse them out of pity, remembering the ignorance of youth, which prevents their having greater knowledge. Good Lord! Consider that if just now you don't have within you the impulses that youth has, and you no longer delight in such follies because of old age, which has mellowed you and cooled you off, you are, however, not without sin; rather you perhaps have more of it and worse than you had at that age or than many young people have. If those particular vices have left you, other worse ones have taken their place, like envy, covetousness, anger, impatience and gluttony (especially of wine, in which you often overindulge). You, who ought to be wise, do not have the power to resist them, because the inclinations of old age attract, tempt and encourage you. And you want these young people to be wiser than you and do what you are unable to do yourself, that is, to resist the temptations that youth puts into their heads. So leave the young people in peace and stop complaining about them, for if you examine yourself well, you have enough to worry about. If the vices of youth have left you, it is not because of your virtue, but because nature no longer inclines you to them, and for that reason they seem to you so abominable that you cannot bear them.'

7. How young women ought to conduct themselves towards their elders.

Now we come to the teachings that will not only prevent young people from arguing with older ones and being contemptuous of them, but also can encourage young people to revere their elders. This is what we say to them.

O children and you young people who are quick to learn and remember, understand this lesson which can introduce you profitably to the manners and customs you ought to observe towards the most honourable estate of the elderly. This lesson will introduce you to five principal points, of which the first concerns the reverence that you should bear them. The second concerns obedience; the third, fear; the fourth, aid and comfort. The fifth point encourages you to consider the good that they do you and the benefits that you have because of them.

As for the first of these points, which is the reverence that you owe them by rights: it is written that there was once a king in Greece called Lycurgus who devised many excellent laws, one of which was that young people should honour and revere the elderly. Now once this king or his successor sent his ambassadors into another land, and some young nobles of the country went with them to guard, serve and accompany them. When the time came to make their representation, there was a great crowd in the place where they were sitting, for the people had assembled there to hear what the ambassadors had to say. All the places were taken. Then an old man came to hear, like the others, and he went searching all around to find a place to sit. No one of his own nation was courteous enough to give him a seat, but when he came to the place where those young foreigners were sitting, they immediately stood up and bowed and according to the laws of their own country gave a seat to the old man. This thing was very widely noted and praised, and everyone esteemed them for it. The Romans likewise had these same customs when they were governed by excellent laws. You children and young people should take this example to heart as a sound doctrine, for you should know that Right and Reason want to have honour accorded to them, and even Holy Scripture bears witness to this. You may be certain that you will be greatly praised for doing this, for honour does not reside only with the person to whom it is done. And if you owe honour to the elderly, it follows that at all costs you must avoid mocking them and doing or saying injurious, derisive or out-rageous things, or bad things of whatever kind. Do not displease or find fault with them, as some wicked young people do who are very much to be reproached for it, who call them 'old boys' or 'old biddies'; this is a clear reproach to one who otherwise conducts herself well.

The second point, which is that you ought to obey them, involves being quite convinced in your own mind that they are wiser than you are. It is to your advantage to abide by the judgement of wise elderly people more than by your own and to make use of their advice and be governed and ruled by them in your most important undertakings. By doing this you will avoid criticism.

The third point is that, although they may not all be strong enough physically to beat you and you may not be afraid of them, you still ought to fear them as though they were all your fathers and mothers. The reason for this is that they have with them (in their common sense and knowledge) a rod of correction for you, and therefore it is proper for you to fear their presence. In other words, you should avoid doing wrong in front of them, for they will notice it.

The fourth point is that you must help them compassionately and comfort them with the strength of your body and with your worldly goods in their illnesses and frailty. In other words, help those who have need of it in humane compassion, remembering that you too will become powerless and weak if you live that long, and then you would surely wish to be comforted yourself. You should also do it for God as the greatest charity and almsgiving that there is, for there is no worse disease than old age.

Then the fifth point, which is to do with the good that you receive through elderly people, which ought to move you all the more to put up with them and have compassion for them, is that they are the ones who established the sciences and even the laws. By them you have been taught and governed by the rule of law, to such a degree that you will never be able to pay them back for these great favours. Every day the elderly also uphold in all lands, countries and kingdoms the fine laws and ordinances of the world. For in spite of the great strength of the young, if it were not for the wise elderly people the world would be in chaos. Holy Scripture bears witness to this very thing, saying, 'Woe betide the land of which the king or lord is a child', that is, immature. You young people ought to conduct yourselves towards the elderly according to these rules so that your good and the good of your reputation itself may increase by it, for a good reputation that is passed on by word of mouth from one wise elderly person to another, who adds to it confidently, is a very sound reputation. If the young who desire a good reputation are well advised, they ought to go to great lengths to be in their favour by good manners, so that elderly people may praise them. This advice that we have given in this passage applies no less to young men than to young women.

But to get back to our subject, the teaching for women: elderly people possess the above-mentioned good sense and advantages, that is, those men and women who are honourable and wise, for we do not mean some unfortunate old people hardened in their sins and vices, in whom there is no sense or goodness whatsoever. These people are to be avoided more than any other living thing, but any young woman who desires honour ought to make friends gladly with the good and respectable ones and happily go to feasts or whatever place in their company, more so than with young women, for she will be more praised for it and she will gain more self-confidence. If something untoward happens at the gathering, then the dishonour or blame will not fall on the one who is in the honourable company of a well-regarded elderly woman. So the young woman, as we have said, ought to serve, honour and bear great reverence towards the elderly woman and be patient with her. Let us suppose that it is somewhat disagreeable or difficult for her to receive her correction with a good grace and not to reply ungraciously: the young woman should either keep quiet or else speak courteously and placate her adroitly if she can and avoid doing the things that she knows can make her angry, and for doing this she will be greatly praised.

If the elderly have this attitude to the young, and the young treat the elderly in this way, the peace can be kept between these two groups, who often are in great discord.

8. Of the wives of artisans and how they ought to conduct themselves.

Now it is time for us to speak of the station in life of women married to artisans who live in cities and fine towns, like Paris, and elsewhere. They can use all the good things that have been said before, but yet some tradesmen like goldsmiths, embroiderers, armourers, tapestry makers and many others are more respectable than are masons, shoemakers and such like. All wives of artisans should be very painstaking and diligent if they wish to have the necessities of life. They should encourage their husbands or their workmen to get to work early in the morning and work until late, for mark our words, there is no trade so good that if you neglect your work you will not have difficulty putting bread on the table. And besides encouraging the others, the wife herself should be involved in the work to the extent that she knows all about it, so that she may know how to oversee his workers if her husband is absent, and to reprove them if they do not do well. She ought to oversee them to keep them from idleness, for through careless workers the master is sometimes ruined. And when customers come to her husband and try to drive a hard bargain, she ought to warn him solicitously to take care that he does not make a bad deal. She should advise him to be chary of giving too much credit if he does not know precisely where and to whom it is going, for in this way many come to poverty, although sometimes the greed to earn more or to accept a tempting proposition makes them do it.

In addition, she ought to keep her husband's love as much as she can, to this end: that he will stay at home more willingly and that he may not have any reason to join the foolish crowds of other young men in taverns and indulge in unnecessary and extravagant expense, as many tradesmen do, especially in Paris. By treating him kindly she should protect him as well as she can from this. It is said that three things drive a man from his home: a quarrelsome wife, a smoking fireplace and a leaking roof. She too ought to stay at home gladly and not go every day traipsing hither and yon gossiping with the neighbours and visiting her chums to find out what everyone is doing. That is done by slovenly housewives roaming about the town in groups. Nor should she go off on these pilgrimages got up for no good reason and involving a lot of needless expense. Furthermore, she ought to remind her husband that they should live so frugally that their expenditure does not exceed their income, so that at the end of the year they do not find themselves in debt.

If she has children, she should have them instructed and taught first at school by educated people so that they may know how better to serve God. Afterwards they may be put to some trade by which they may earn a living, for whoever gives a trade or business training to her child gives a great possession. The children should be kept from wantonness and from voluptuousness above all else, for truly it is something that most shames the children of good towns and is a great sin of mothers and fathers, who ought to be the cause of the virtue and good behaviour of their children, but they are sometimes the reason (because of bringing them up to be finicky and indulging them too much) for their wickedness and ruin.

9. Of servant-women and chambermaids.

So that everyone may benefit from our advice on living well, we will speak even to servant-women and chambermaids of Paris and elsewhere. As in many places the necessity of earning their living causes many of them to be put quite young to serve, the occupation of secular service has perhaps prevented them from knowing as thoroughly as other people things that concern the salvation of their souls. They may not know as much about serving God by hearing Masses and sermons and saying Our Fathers and other prayers, which some good women would like to do, but their serving duties do not allow them.

It seems a good idea to say a little about the manner in deed, work and thought that is advantageous for them to have for their salvation, and also something about what they ought to avoid. Any servant-woman ought to know that she can be excused, even by God, for not doing things for which her mistress or another lady of leisure would not be excused. For example, if she is in service because of the necessity of earning a living and in order to perform her service better she must work very hard, rise early and go to bed late, dine and sup after everyone else and with scarcely the time for it, but go about eating here and there all the time in the midst of her duties – and perhaps she will not get very much to eat, but a rather scanty amount and catch as catch can – if such a woman does not fast on all the days ordained by the Church, God will excuse her. Indeed, she may feel that she cannot do it without harming her health, which might perhaps be damaged so that she could not earn her living. But she should not break her fast out of gluttony and foolish presumption, saying, 'I am a servant. I don't have to fast.' Discretion and a good conscience ought to determine the right thing to do and be the judges of the matter, for there are chambermaids with more leisure in all respects than many housewives who fast for the love of God; what we say does not apply to those women. Likewise we advise going into the church and praying.

But what should the good servant-woman do to deserve salvation? Certainly she ought to understand that God, who knows and sees everything, asks only that she have a good heart towards Him, for then she cannot go wrong. The one who has a good heart will be saved and thereby will protect herself from all odious and wicked sins. She will be loyal in deed and in word to master and mistress and will serve them with care, and even while doing her duties she will be able to say her Our Fathers and her devotions. If she is prevented from getting to church, she can be there in spirit, although it is scarcely to be believed that anyone is so busy that if she wanted to take the trouble to get up early she could not easily find the time on most days to hear a Mass and recommend herself to God, and then come back to do her chores. If she adopts such a course, together with the other good deeds that a good serving-woman can do, these things will inevitably lead her to salvation.

But to behave as some debauched and wicked women do is the

road to damnation! In order to reprimand them for their follies and wicked ways let us say this: there are some dishonest chambermaids who are given great responsibility because they know how to insinuate themselves into the great houses of the middle classes and of rich people by cleverly acting the part of good household managers. They get their position of buying the food and going to the butcher's, where they only too well 'hit the fruit basket', which is a common expression meaning to claim that the thing costs more than it really does and then keep the change. So they pretend that a piece of mutton costs them four *sous* that they got for ten *blancs* or less, and so on with other things, and in this way they can do great harm over a period of a year. For they put to one side a little titbit, have a pie made and baked, charging it up to their master, and then when their master is at court or in town, and their mistress at church hearing high Mass, a delightful little banquet is spread in the kitchen, and not without plenty to drink, and only the best wine! The other housemaids in the street who are part of the crowd of cronies turn up, and God knows how they plunder the place! Someone takes the pie to the room she has in the town and her paramour comes over, and they have a merry time together.

There may be women who frequent the house and help to do the laundry or scour the pots who are in cahoots with the housemaid, and so they do the work of the household while she loafs, so that the master and the mistress find everything in order when they come home, but God knows how cheated they are of wine and food! Or sometimes, when the laundry is done at home, the mistress, preoccupied with something else, will think that her maid is at the river to wash her laundry, but instead she is at the baths in peace and ease, and has her friends doing her work for her. She does not pay them or her relatives and her pals who sometimes come asking for her at the house and wanting to see her, but God knows that the relatives and the many cronies she has in the town cost the house many bottles of wine!

If such a woman serves in some place where there is a young newly married mistress who is a bit silly, she is on to a good thing. She will know how to flatter the master and speak to him as an equal and fawn on him so that he has confidence in her about his wife and about everything else. But she will always pull the wool over his eyes! On the other hand she will also flatter the girl, so that in this way she will have them both believing that she is practically the

Messiah! And then wine and food, candles, bread, salted pork, salt and every other staple of the house will be very well taken care of indeed, and if the master sometimes says that the provisions run out too quickly, she will have her answer ready, saying that it is because they give too many big dinner parties and invite so many people to drink. But if some gallant promises to give, or does give, her a cloak or a gown for taking a message to her mistress, if she does not do it discreetly, the mistress could be burnt! Such greedy housemaids can pose a very great danger in a house, for because of the excellent service that they know how to give, and their flatteries, and by preparing meals well, keeping the house neat and clean, and speaking well and answering questions politely, they blind people so much that no one is on the look-out for their wicked deeds. The better to cover up everything, they pretend to be pious and go to church for all the prayers, and therein lies the danger.

So you ladies who have servants, watch out for these tricks so that you are not deceived. And to you who serve, we say this so that you may regard doing such things as an abomination, for inevitably those who do them damn themselves and deserve death of both body and soul, for because of people like this, many are burnt or buried alive who do not deserve it.*

10. Of the instruction for prostitutes.

Just as the sun shines on the just and on the unjust, we have no shame in extending our instruction even to the women who are foolish and loose and lead disorderly lives, although there is nothing more abominable. Nor should we feel any shame, recalling that Jesus Christ Himself felt no repugnance in showing such women the error of their ways and turning them away from sin. Therefore, for charity and goodness and so that some of them may perhaps retain from our teachings something that may rescue them from their disreputable lives, we will teach them something. A greater act of charity cannot be performed than to rescue a sinner from evil and from sin.

We say this to you: you miserable women so indecently given to sin, open your eyes with recognition. Go back while you have the light of day and before you are surprised by nightfall, in other words,

---

* These punishments were sometimes the penalties for adultery.

while life remains in your body and so that death does not assail you and seize you in sin that leads you to Hell, for no one knows the hour of his end. Consider the great filth of your way of life, so abominable that besides your being the object of God's wrath, the world also disdains you. All decent persons flee from you as an excommunicated thing, and in the street look away so that they will not see you. Why does such a foul character exist in you that people talk of such abomination? You thus sunk in sin, how can a woman degenerate into such vice, who by her nature and upbringing is decent, mild and modest? How can she tolerate indecency and living, drinking and eating entirely among men more vile than swine – men who strike her, drag her about and threaten her, and by whom she is always in danger of being killed? Alas, why have womanly mildness and decency degenerated in you to such low and vulgar behaviour? Oh, in the name of God, you women who bear the name of Christianity and who pervert it in such foul pursuits, raise yourselves, arise from this abominable mud and refuse to allow your poor souls to be loaded down with filth committed by your lowly bodies. An all-pitying God is prepared to receive you mercifully if you want to repent and ask contritely for mercy. Take as your example the blessed Mary of Egypt, who repented of her misguided life and turned to God and is a glorious saint in Paradise. Likewise the blessed St Afra, who offered her body, with which she had sinned, to martyrdom for the honour of Our Lord, and others similarly who have been saved. Some of you may wish to excuse yourselves, saying that you would gladly do it, but three reasons hinder you: first, because your disreputable customers would not let you; second, that the world in revulsion would reject you and ostracize you, and for that reason you would be so ashamed that you would never dare to be seen among ordinary people; third, that you would not have a way of making a living, for you do not know a trade.

We say that these arguments are worthless, for there is a solution to every problem. You ought to know that without doubt no woman is so low that if she sincerely wishes to renounce sin with the good intention of never returning to it or falling again, if she repents and begs God's mercy, God will protect and preserve her from all those who wish to dissuade her from her good intentions. But she herself, if she wishes to keep from sin in deed and appearance, must get rid of her very indecent clothing and dress herself in long and modest gowns and stay away from the haunts that she used to frequent. She must go to chapel and church, pray devoutly, follow the sermons with piety and confess with great repentance to a wise confessor. To all those who would reproach her for sin, she should reply simply that she would sooner offer her body to martyrdom than sin, for God has given her the grace to repent and renounce it, so she will never go back to it for anything in the world. And by adopting this course there is no doubt (calling God to her aid) that she can be freed of any debauchery, no matter how great, and if she then finds some bad person whom she cannot resist, immediately she must tell her problem to a magistrate, who will take pity on her, and she will be resolute.

As for the second excuse, which is that the world would despise her: she ought not to have such an opinion, nor give up because of this, for the truth is quite the opposite, and she need have no doubt that all who see her reformed and ashamed of her sin and dissolute life will feel very great pity for her. They will welcome her with open arms, say kind things to her, and give her occasion to persevere and do well. She will be seen to have such a good and respectable life, such a devout and humble manner, that while she used to be rebuffed by everyone she will now be befriended and cherished by all good people. And so by doing good and by the grace of God, she will have recovered her honour through shame. And why might she not? When God has pardoned her and taken her into grace, there would be no reason for the world to reject her. Without a doubt, any woman given to shame and sin should certainly wish to achieve this reformed state, and that would come about if she wished it to.

The third excuse, which is that she would have no livelihood, counts for nothing, for if she has a strong and able body for doing evil and suffering many beatings and misfortunes, she could just as well use it for earning her living, and if she were so disposed, everyone would gladly take her to help do the laundry in their big houses. They would take pity on her and gladly give her a means of making a living, but she must take care that no one ever sees anything foul or wicked in her. She could spin or look after the sick and women in child-bed, while living in a little room in a good street and among good people. She would live there simply and soberly, so that she was never seen drunk or aggressive or quarrelsome or brawling. She would be very careful that not one word of lubricity or indecency issued from her mouth; she would always be courteous, humble, kind and amiable to all good people. She would have to avoid the attentions of men, for otherwise she would lose everything. By means of this course of action she would be able both to serve God and earn her living, so one penny earned in this way would do her more good than a hundred received in sin.

11. *In praise of respectable and chaste women.*

Just as white differs from black, and when they are put side by side the difference is more noticeable, so we have chosen, in order to give more space to respectable and chaste women, to speak to them now. We will praise them, not to make them vain, but so that perseverance in doing good may be a pleasure to them and that all women will wish to be in their ranks. So we mention them after what we have said to the poor sinners, for just as these lost ones can raise themselves by the grace of God, change their ways and be saved, the good women also could be deflected from the right course by the temptation of the devil and their own weakness and so be destroyed and damned, for the constancy of the good pilgrim is not known until the very end of his journey. For this reason, considering poor human fragility, soon apt to stumble, no one ought to presume that he is stronger than St Peter was or than David and Solomon were, and others of great knowledge who have fallen into sin. This is our message to you respectable women who live chastely.

Affectionate greetings, dear friends. The pleasure that we take in praising chastity induces us to write to you about both the characteristics of this noble flower and the praises that are bestowed upon it, to the end that, just as the more a good workman is praised for his good work the more he enjoys doing good work, you may do likewise. Although we could hardly list all its virtues, nevertheless we want to reiterate briefly certain outstanding ones.

Chastity has the property of rendering the person who has it agreeable before God; without it a person would not be able to please Him and he would perish, according to what St Ambrose asserts when he says that chastity turns a human being into an angel. St Bernard agrees with this opinion, saying that there can be no lovelier thing than chastity, which can make an agreeable dwelling for God out of a human being conceived of semen and vile matter and in sin. 'Chastity,' he says, 'is the only virtue which in this mortal world represents the immortality of the higher one, that is, that the persons who have it in them can be compared to the holy spirits of Heaven.

Infinite are the qualities and praises that the Holy Scriptures record of this celestial virtue.' And besides its being so highly regarded by God, experience shows us that it is likewise highly praised in the world, for there is no one so full of faults that if it is generally known that she is chaste people will not respect her, but if she has the opposite reputation, regardless of her good deeds she cannot avoid being mocked behind her back and respected less.

So, therefore, may you women of good repute continue to take pleasure in your chastity, but not to suggest deceitfully by gestures and words that you are chaste when secretly the opposite may be in you, for God, from whom nothing is hidden, would know it very well, and would punish you for it, but in honest truth may your conscience be clear. Do not do as some foolish women do who try to hide their follies by talking about other people, or claiming that they themselves are highly respectable women, and that they abominate such a deed. Such an attitude invites scorn, for however good a woman may be, the better she is the more seemly it is for her to keep silent in this situation, because she ought to assume that other women are similarly chaste. There is no proof that she herself is chaste when she finds things to say about the others, and so in this situation she should give others the benefit of the doubt. You should not pride yourself on your chastity, mocking and feeling superior to other women, even supposing that you definitely know about their vices. Do not speak badly of them in order to vaunt yourself and show that you are better.

There are two reasons for this. The first is that you do not know what is to happen to you nor how tempted you will be, for as the common proverb says: 'When the sheep is old the wolf can still sometimes carry it off.' The other reason is that if you do not have that particular sin, you perhaps have other ones even worse in God's eyes, as we have mentioned previously in this book, although they may perchance not be so dishonourable in the opinion of the world. You ought to have pity on fallen women, pray for them, give them a chance to redeem themselves, and praise God for saving you from such wickedness. You ought to pray to Him to give you perseverance. You must avoid the occasions that could tempt you to sin and keep yourselves humble towards God. Do not be proud of yourselves, but always be meek, and by holding to this course you can drive your chariot up to the farthest reaches of glory that Almighty God bestows upon you.

12. Of the wives of labourers.

Now we must draw towards the end of our project, speaking to simple labouring women in the villages. It is not necessary to prohibit fancy ornaments or extravagant clothing to them, for they are well protected from these excesses! Although they are commonly raised on black bread, salt pork and gruel, with only water to drink, and they work very hard, their lives are more secure and more abundant in essentials than the lives of some who are placed very high. And because every person of whatever rank he or she may be needs an introduction to right living, we are pleased to have them share in our lessons. This is our message to them.

Listen, simple women who live in villages, in low country or in mountains, who cannot often hear what the Church prescribes to every person for his salvation through what your curate or chaplain might tell you Sunday after Sunday. We will put it briefly: remember our lessons addressed to you, if it happens to reach your ears, so that ignorance, which can deceive you through lack of knowing more, will not deprive you of salvation. You ought to know first of all that there is one all-powerful God, all-good, all-just and all-wise, from whom nothing is hidden, who rewards every person, either with something good or something bad, according to what he has deserved. He alone must be perfectly loved and served. But because He is so good that He welcomes all service that a good heart presents to Him, and so wise that He knows the potential of everyone, it is enough for Him that each person behaves towards Him sincerely and according to his abilities. For this reason you who must help the world with your labour, which is for the sustenance, life and nourishment of every human being, cannot vacate your post or try to serve Him by making fasts, saying prayers or going to church like other women in large towns. However, you also need salvation as much as the others, and so you must therefore serve Him in another way, as we will tell you: that is, in heart and will. That is, inasmuch as you love Him with all your heart, you must avoid doing to your neighbours or other people what you would not wish them to do to you.

And remind your husbands of this – that is, when they are working on the land for another person, they should do it as well and as faithfully as if they were doing it for themselves. If it is harvest time, they must pay their master with the wheat that has grown on the land (if that is the arrangement) and not mix rye with the wheat and claim that it is otherwise. They should not hide the good lambs nor the best sheep at the neighbours' or elsewhere so that they can pay the master with the worst ones when he comes for the sharing-out; nor should they pretend that his sheep are dead nor show him the hides of other animals, nor pay him with the worst fleeces. The men must not render false accounts for the master's waggons, or his fowl or anything else of his. The wives should remind their husbands not to cut wood to build their houses from somebody else's forest without permission. When they tend the grapevines, they must be diligent to do the work thoroughly and at the right time of the year. When they are entrusted by their masters to engage other workers, if they are hired for six *blancs* per day, they should not pretend that the rate was seven. The good wives should advise their husbands about all such things, so that they may avoid them, for otherwise they will be damned.

By doing their work well and faithfully, they will have grace in their lives, and they will undoubtedly be saved; their lives will be good and acceptable to God. The wives themselves ought to help them in whatever ways they can and take care not to go, nor to allow their children to go, and break down the hedges to steal grapes from someone else's garden at night (or in the daytime either) nor other people's fruits or any garden produce or anything else. They must not pasture their livestock in their neighbours' meadows. They should not take anything at all away from another person that they would not want taken from themselves. They should go to church as much as they can, and pay their tithes faithfully to God (and not the worst things) and say their Our Fathers. They should live in peace with their neighbours without going to law over every little dispute, as quite a few village people do, who are not happy if they are not suing someone. They should believe in God, and have pity on those they see suffering. By keeping to these paths, good people may be saved, both men and women.

13. *Of the condition of poor people.*

As we began with the rich and then spoke to all classes of women, it is fitting that we end our work with the class that God loves but the world hates – the poor, both men and women. We exhort them to patience because of the hope of the crown that is promised them, saying: O blessed poor, by the judgement of God recorded in the

Gospels, waiting for the possession of Heaven by the merit of poverty patiently borne, rejoice in this great promise of joy which surpasses everything else and to which no other rich possession can be compared! It is not promised to kings, princes or the rich if they are not of your spiritual kingdom, that is, poor of spirit, unless they disdain worldly riches and frivolities and do not love them. Dearest friends loved by God, please remember our advice, if it can come to your notice and remind you of what can help you against the stings of impatience when they attack you with the various and very great afflictions that you bear, namely frequent hunger and thirst, cold, poor shelter, a friendless old age, sickness without comfort, and besides that, the contempt, villainy and rejection of the world, as if you were another race of humans and not Christians. When the stings of this impatience assail you, so that you do not, through it, lose the aforementioned great treasures that are promised to you, may the Lady Hope come, loved by Patience, with the shield of Faith, who fights powerfully against impatience.

To vanquish it and give you the victory, she attacks it with these five spears. The first that she will throw at it is this: 'O poor sinner, what ails you? You who complain of poverty, is there any man in the world who would not hold himself well recompensed to be dressed in the king's livery? ("O my Creator, Almighty King above all kings, I Your poor created being who am dressed in Your garments in soul and in body, have no value in my soul except as You have made it in Your image. In body I have human flesh, as You wanted to have, dressed in poverty, the garment You wanted to wear all Your life. You show very clearly how You dignified the condition of poverty more than any other when You chose it for Yourself. Now, it is obvious that Your judgements are not like those of human beings, for who was ever in this world poorer than You when You chose to be born in a poor obscure stable among dumb beasts in the winter-time, swaddled in rags? Who could have been poorer than You, who elected to spend all Your life in such poverty that You never had anything of Your own except what You were given as alms? You often suffered hunger, thirst and every misery, chose to die and be tormented completely naked, and were so poor that You did not even have a pillow on which to rest Your worthy head. Alas, miserable creature that I am, ought I to complain of being like You? Lord God, I thank You for having deigned to honour me so much, for You want me by the temporary hunger that I now endure and suffer to be seated on high at Your holy table forever. So I am content and wish, my Lord, that Your holy will may be done.")'

The second spear that she will throw will be this: 'And if you are now ill and with little comfort, God wishes it, so that through the patience with which you endure it your merit may be all the greater.'

The third spear is: 'If you are old and have no friends, of what importance to you would these friends be? What would they do for you? Certainly they would never relieve you of your old age, nor would they increase your merit. The older you are, aged and in decline, the better it is for you. You are closer to the end of your journey and to your God and Creator, who by His holy mercy (if you are patient) will restore your strength, power and youth, and all glory and happiness, just as He has promised to all His loyal servants.'

The fourth spear is: 'If you are now lying on a dunghill or a bit of straw (which has to last you for only a very short time) or in a poor and uncomfortable dwelling where you hardly have the necessities of life, what misfortune is it for you, considering the blessed dwelling in Paradise, beautiful and delightful beyond anything else, where you will lack for nothing? Remember that your present misery is not permanent.'

The fifth spear is: 'If the world scorns or rejects you, you are well injured! Consider what the worldly honours they had during their lifetimes are worth now to the kings, great people and the rich who are now dead. Alas, there is no doubt that those honours have been the cause of damning many who would have been better off to be in your situation.'

By these spears and by accepting your poverty willingly, having faith in God and not desiring anything except what pleases Him, you poor and indigent women can conquer and overcome the attacks of impatience, which are not small when they come through great oppression of necessity. By means of this course of action you can acquire nobler possessions and more riches than a hundred thousand worlds could contain, and they are everlasting. You therefore have cause to regard everything as a reason for praising God for the worldly position to which He has called you, although it may be hard to bear. You good and poor women who have your poor husbands, you must comfort them with these precepts; help one another as best you can. Poor widows also should be comforted by God, waiting for the eternal joy that God gives you.

We recommend you to God, Christine, dear friend. And so we leave our work.

The end and conclusion of this book.

With that the three ladies stopped speaking and suddenly disappeared, and I, Christine, remained, almost exhausted from writing for so long, but very happy, looking at the beautiful work of their worthy lessons, which I have recapitulated. The more I look at them the better they seem: very profitable for the good, the improvement of virtuous habits, and the increase of honour of ladies and the whole world of women, present and future, wherever this book can reach and be seen. And therefore I, their servant (although I am not always capable of busying myself in their service, albeit I continually desire it), thought to myself that I would distribute many copies of this work throughout the world whatever the cost, and it would be presented in various places to queens, princesses and great ladies, so that it might be more honoured and exalted, for it is worthy of it, and it might be spread among other women. This idea would ensure its being issued and circulated in all countries. As it is in the French tongue and as that language is more common throughout the world than any other, this work will not remain useless and forgotten. It will endure in many copies all over the world without falling into disuse, and many valiant ladies and women of authority will see and hear it now and in time to come.

May they pray to God for their servant Christine, desiring that they may see her life in this world last as long as their own. May it please them all to remember her kindly with friendly greetings as long as she lives, praying to God that by His pity she may be judged with increasing favour and that He may give her such light of knowledge and true wisdom that she may be able to use it here below in the noble labour of study and the exaltation of virtue in good examples to every human being. And after her soul is parted from the body in merit and reward for its service, let them offer paternosters, oblations and devotions to God for her for the easing of the pains she has deserved for her faults, so that she may be presented before God, world without end, given us by the Father, Son and Holy Ghost. Amen.

FOR THE BEST IN PAPERBACKS, LOOK FOR THE

In every corner of the world, on every subject under the sun, Penguin represents quality and variety – the very best in publishing today.

For complete information about books available from Penguin – including Pelicans, Puffins, Peregrines and Penguin Classics – and how to order them, write to us at the appropriate address below. Please note that for copyright reasons the selection of books varies from country to country.

In the United Kingdom: Please write to *Dept E.P., Penguin Books Ltd, Harmondsworth, Middlesex, UB7 0DA*

If you have any difficulty in obtaining a title, please send your order with the correct money, plus ten per cent for postage and packaging, to *PO Box No 11, West Drayton, Middlesex*

In the United States: Please write to *Dept BA, Penguin, 299 Murray Hill Parkway, East Rutherford, New Jersey 07073*

In Canada: Please write to *Penguin Books Canada Ltd, 2801 John Street, Markham, Ontario L3R 1B4*

In Australia: Please write to the *Marketing Department, Penguin Books Australia Ltd, P.O. Box 257, Ringwood, Victoria 3134*

In New Zealand: Please write to the *Marketing Department, Penguin Books (NZ) Ltd, Private Bag, Takapuna, Auckland 9*

In India: Please write to *Penguin Overseas Ltd, 706 Eros Apartments, 56 Nehru Place, New Delhi, 110019*

In Holland: Please write to *Penguin Books Nederland B.V., Postbus 195, NL–1380AD Weesp, Netherlands*

In Germany: Please write to *Penguin Books Ltd, Friedrichstrasse 10–12, D–6000 Frankfurt Main 1, Federal Republic of Germany*

In Spain: Please write to *Longman Penguin España, Calle San Nicolas 15, E–28013 Madrid, Spain*

In France: Please write to *Penguin Books Ltd, 39 Rue de Montmorency, F-75003, Paris, France*

In Japan: Please write to *Longman Penguin Japan Co Ltd, Yamaguchi Building, 2–12–9 Kanda Jimbocho, Chiyoda-Ku, Tokyo 101, Japan*

WOLFRAM VON ESCHENBACH
PARZIVAL
Translated by A. T. Hatto

In *Parzival*, one of the world's greatest narrative poems, Wolfram von Eschenbach (*fl. c.* 1195–1225) retells and ends the Arthurian *Story of the Grail*, left unfinished by its initiator Chrétien de Troyes.

Against alternating backgrounds of dazzling courtly ritual and the forbidding landscapes of the wilds is displayed Parzival's exemplary quest for the supreme goal of chivalry, the spiritual aspects of which are dramatized by juxtaposition of the more happy-go-lucky careers of Parzival's father and his amorous comrade-in-arms Gawan.

THE NIBELUNGENLIED
Translated by A. T. Hatto

Composed nearly eight hundred years ago by an unnamed poet, *The Nibelungenlied* is the principal literary expression of those heroic legends of which Richard Wagner made such free use in *The Ring*. This great German epic poem of murder and revenge recounts with peculiar strength and directness the progress Siegfried's love for peerless Kriemhild, the wedding of Gunther and Brunhild, the quarrel between the two queens, Hagen's treacherous murder of Siegfried, and Kriemhild's eventual revenge. A. T. Hatto's new translation transforms an old text into a story as readable and exciting as Homer's *Iliad*.

THE MABINOGION
Translated by Jeffrey Gantz

'On the bank of the river he saw a tall tree: from roots to crown one half was aflame and the other green with leaves.'

Nothing illustrates the strange nature of these Welsh stories better than this vertically halved tree. The combination of fact and fantasy, of myth, history and folklore in *The Mabinogion* conjures up a magical enchanted world, which is nonetheless firmly rooted in the forests, hills and valleys of ancient Wales. The eleven stories were composed orally over a span of centuries, before being written down in the thirteenth century; they represent, in their virtuosity and panache, one of the high points of the Welsh imagination.

A CELTIC MISCELLANY
Translated by Kenneth Hurlstone Jackson

This well-known anthology of Irish, Scottish, Gaelic, Manx, Welsh, Cornish and Breton literature (now thoroughly revised for the Penguin Classics) is more representative than most collections because it draws on the prose as well as the poetry of the Celtic languages. The feats of the legendary hero Cú Chulainn and the infectious ribaldry of the fourteenth-century poet Dafydd ap Gwilym combine with epigrams, tales of 'Celtic magic', descriptive passages, Bardic poetry, laments and poems of love and nature to reflect the whole spectrum of Celtic imagination, from the earliest times to the nineteenth century.

THE PENGUIN CLASSICS

THE EARLIEST ENGLISH POEMS
Translated by Michael Alexander

As a literary language Anglo-Saxon seemingly died after the Norman Conquest; in the mouths of ordinary people, however, it survived to become the tap-root of the language we speak.

Preserving the original metre and alliteration Michael Alexander has translated the best Anglo-Saxon poetry into modern English. In addition to passages from *Beowulf*, this anthology includes, amongst other poems, *Widsith*, *Deor*, *The Wanderer*, *The Seafarer*, and *The Battle of Maldon*. Together these fairly represent a body of alliterative poetry which, at its best, moves with a sad and stately nobility of its own.

BEOWULF
Translated by Michael Alexander

Beowulf is the most important Old English poem and perhaps the most significant single survival from the Anglo-Saxon period. Though its composition was completed in England in the eighth century, the poem is set in the heroic societies of a fifth-century Scandinavia.

We have here something more than merely a heroic poem of historical interest: *Beowulf* has a truly epic quality and scope, and this new verse translation successfully communicates this poem's artistry and eloquence.

THE PENGUIN CLASSICS

BEROUL
THE ROMANCE OF TRISTAN
Translated by A. T. Hatto

The tragic story of the illicit passion of Tristan and Yseut, which brought them only degradation, has lost none of its fascination since it was first composed about the middle of the twelfth century. Beroul's poem is perhaps the earliest version of the legend now extant, and the poet presents his narration in an abrupt, jerky style well suited to the violence and brutality of his matter. Of all the poets who have treated the *Tristan* legend, Beroul, about whom nothing at all is known, comes closest to preserving that elemental drive which is the very essence of the story and which has given it such tremendous vitality in the literature of western civilization.

GOTTFRIED VON STRASSBURG
TRISTAN
Translated by A. T. Hatto

'If the two of whom this love-story tells had not endured sorrow for the sake of joy, love's pain for its ecstasy within one heart, their name and history would never have brought such rapture to so many noble spirits.'

Gottfried von Strassburg's *Tristan* (c. 1210), here completed with the surviving fragments of the earlier *Tristan* of Thomas, is a masterpiece of formal artistry. This tale of the hero Tristan and the beautiful Queen Isolde, united by a magic potion in a passion that defies all legal and moral sanctions, has stood the test of time as one of the greatest love-stories ever written.

THE PENGUIN CLASSICS

MEDIEVAL ENGLISH VERSE
Translated by Brian Stone

This is an anthology of modern verse translations of English poetry of the thirteenth and fourteenth centuries. In a very full selection about half the space is devoted to short poems, including religious and secular lyrics as well as moral, political, polemical and comic verse. The other half contains short narrative poems, and of these 'Pearl', the longest and most important, ranks among the finest elegies in English. In addition to 'Patience', a minor epic, and 'Sir Orfeo', defined as a Breton lay, the collection includes a rollicking example of medieval bawdry, 'Dame Siriz and the Weeping Bitch'.

THE OWL AND THE NIGHTINGALE
CLEANNESS
ST ERKENWALD
Translated by Brian Stone

The Middle English poems in this book exemplify three major genres in medieval religious writing: saint's legend, Bible epic and religious debate. *St Erkenwald*, perhaps the best saint's legend in English poetry, tells how a bishop of London raised a pagan judge from the dead and sent his soul to heaven. In *Cleanness* (often known as *Purity*) such events as the Flood, the destruction of Sodom and Gomorrah and Belshazzar's feast are recounted with the descriptive eloquence of the poet who wrote *Sir Gawain and the Green Knight*. *The Owl and the Nightingale* is a charming, if occasionally virulent, contest between two birds who debate, owl-wise and nightingale-wise, the traditional morals of the church and the ideals of courtly love.

LANGLAND
PIERS THE PLOUGHMAN
Translated by J. F. Goodridge

Piers the Ploughman, the work of an unknown minor cleric of the late fourteenth century, was perhaps the most widely read work of its day and is now recognized as the great representative English poem of the late Middle Ages. While it offers a vivid picture of fourteenth-century life and is placed firmly in the world of every day, its theme is the pilgrimage of man's soul in search of ultimate truth. Alone among English poets, Langland combines satirical comedy with a rare power of prophecy and vision.

SIR GAWAIN AND THE GREEN KNIGHT
Translated by Brian Stone

Sir Gawain and the Green Knight is the masterpiece of medieval alliterative poetry. The unknown fourteenth-century author (a contemporary of Chaucer) has imbued his work with the heroic atmosphere of a saga, with the spirit of French romance, and with a Christian consciousness. It is a poem in which the virtues of a knight, Sir Gawain, triumphant in almost insuperable ordeals, are celebrated to the glory of the House of Arthur. The impact made on the reader is both magical and human, full of drama and descriptive beauty.

NJAL'S SAGA
*Translated by Magnus Magnusson
and Hermann Pálsson*

Njal's Saga, written by an unknown author in the late thirteenth century, is the mightiest of the great Icelandic prose sagas. Based on historical events in Iceland some 300 years earlier it describes a fifty-year blood feud from its violent beginnings to its tragic end. The spare, simple narrative centres loosely upon the prophetic Njal Thorgeirsson who, with his family, is finally burnt alive in his home by a league of enemies. This translation by Magnus Magnusson and Hermann Pálsson illuminates for us a grim world in which justice means vengeance and all men are either lucky or doomed.

THE VINLAND SAGAS
THE NORSE DISCOVERY
OF AMERICA
*Translated by Magnus Magnusson
and Hermann Pálsson*

The two medieval Icelandic sagas translated in this volume tell one of the most fascinating stories in the history of exploration – the discovery of America by Norsemen, five centuries before Christopher Columbus. In spare and vigorous prose they record Europe's first surprised glimpse of the eastern shores of the North American continent and the Red Indian natives who inhabited them. The Sagas describe how Eirik the Red founded an Icelandic colony in Greenland and how his son, Leif the Lucky, later sailed south to explore and if possible exploit the chance discovery by Bjarni Herjolfsson of an unknown land.

THE PENGUIN CLASSICS

LAXDAELA SAGA

*Translated by Magnus Magnusson
and Hermann Pálsson*

Of all the great medieval Icelandic sagas, *Laxdaela Saga* (composed by an unknown author *c.* 1245) has always stirred the European imagination the most profoundly. Romantic in style, in taste and in theme, it culminates in that most enduring and timeless of human relationships in story-telling, the love triangle. Gudrun Osvif's-daughter, the imperious beauty who is forced to marry her lover's best friend, is one of the first great romantic literary heroines.

With its clerical religious learning, its courtly chivalry, its antiquarian feeling for history and its sympathy for the old heroic poetry, *Laxdaela Saga* reflects European tastes and preoccupations. But it is also intended as a national epic, giving dignity and grandeur to a young nation's past.

HRAFNKEL'S SAGA

Translated by Hermann Pálsson

All seven stories in this volume date from the thirteenth century, and exemplify the outstanding qualities of realistic fiction in medieval Iceland. Falling into two distinctive groups, three of the stories – *Hrafnkel's Saga*, *Thorstein the Staff-Struck*, and *Ale Hood* – are set in the pastoral society of native Iceland; the homely touch and stark realism giving the incidents a strong feeling of immediacy. The remaining four – *Hreidar the Fool*, *Halldor Sorrason*, *Audun's Story*, and *Ivar's Story* – were written without first-hand knowledge of Scandinavia, and describe the adventures of Icelandic poets and peasants at the royal courts of Norway and Denmark.

ORKNEYINGA SAGA

THE HISTORY OF THE EARLS OF ORKNEY

Translated by Hermann Pálsson and Paul Edwards

Probably written around A.D. 1200 the *Orkneyinga Saga* is the only Norse saga concerned with what is now part of the British Isles. Beginning in the remote world of mythic origins and legends, it relates the conquest of the Northern Scottish Isles by the kings of Norway during the great Viking expansion of the ninth century and the subsequent history of the Earldom of Orkney.

EGIL'S SAGA

Translated by Hermann Pálsson and Paul Edwards

Egil's Saga offers a panoramic view of the Viking world from the middle of the ninth century to the end of the tenth. However, wide-ranging though it is in time and place, the *Saga* is dominated throughout by the demonic presence of its hero, Egil Skallagrimsson, and the influence of his god, the many-faced Odin – shape-changer and rune-master.

FOR THE BEST IN PAPERBACKS, LOOK FOR THE 🐧

PENGUIN CLASSICS

Saint Anselm	**The Prayers and Meditations**
Saint Augustine	**The Confessions**
Bede	**A History of the English Church and People**
Chaucer	**The Canterbury Tales**
	Love Visions
	Troilus and Criseyde
Froissart	**The Chronicles**
Geoffrey of Monmouth	**The History of the Kings of Britain**
Gerald of Wales	**History and Topography of Ireland**
	The Journey through Wales and The Description of Wales
Gregory of Tours	**The History of the Franks**
Julian of Norwich	**Revelations of Divine Love**
William Langland	**Piers the Ploughman**
Sir John Mandeville	**The Travels of Sir John Mandeville**
Marguerite de Navarre	**The Heptameron**
Christine de Pisan	**The Treasure of the City of Ladies**
Marco Polo	**The Travels**
Richard Rolle	**The Fire of Love**
Thomas à Kempis	**The Imitation of Christ**

ANTHOLOGIES AND ANONYMOUS WORKS

The Age of Bede
Alfred the Great
Beowulf
A Celtic Miscellany
The Cloud of Unknowing and Other Works
The Death of King Arthur
The Earliest English Poems
Early Christian Writings
Early Irish Myths and Sagas
Egil's Saga
The Letters of Abelard and Heloise
Medieval English Verse
Njal's Saga
Seven Viking Romances
Sir Gawain and the Green Knight
The Song of Roland